THE BOOK OF RUMI

THE BOOK OF RUMI

105 Stories and Fables that Illumine, Delight, and Inform

translated by

MARYAM MAFI

foreword by Narguess Farzad

AMARYLLIS

AMARYLLIS
An imprint of Manjul Publishing House Pvt. Ltd.
•7/32, Ansari Road, Daryaganj, New Delhi 110 002
Website: www.manjulindia.com
Registered Office:
•10, Nishat Colony, Bhopal 462 003 – India

Published by arrangement with
Hampton Roads Publishing Company, Inc., USA.

ISBN 978-93-88241-78-6

Cover art: One of a series of paintings of birds and fruit,
Wang Guochen (late 19th century) / School of Oriental and
African Studies Library, University of London /
Bridgeman Images

Book design by Kathryn Sky-Peck

This edition first published in 2019
Second impression 2020

Printed and bound in India by Thomson Press (India) Ltd.

For Mahsima and Alexandre,
the light of my eyes and much more . . .

CONTENTS

MASNAVI I

MASNAVI II

MASNAVI III

MASNAVI IV

MASNAVI V

MASNAVI VI

FOREWORD

Philip Pullman, the Carnegie Medal winner and internationally celebrated author of novels including the trilogy His Dark Materials, has remarked that "after nourishment, shelter and companionship, stories are the thing we need most in the world."

Whatever our cultural or linguistic background, we can all claim some knowledge of the lives of others, and this knowledge has reached us through stories. These stories may have been told by an animated grandparent; maybe we heard them on the radio or encountered them during a religious-studies lesson at school, where we learned about the lives and times of saints, gods, and goddesses.

The literature and history classes that have made the longest-lasting impressions on me are those in which I was allowed a glimpse of the life story of a writer or when my teacher focused on the human stories of the period being taught, peeling away the layers to reveal something of the ordinary life or emotional experiences of the towering figures whose conquests or defeats we were studying or, more poignantly, about the ordinary lives and emotional experiences of the common people of the time. It really did not matter whether these peripheral accounts were tenuous or apocryphal, since their inclusion in the lesson made the whole episode under scrutiny more gripping and memorable.

Stories need not always refer to the great or the good or the legendary. In our own daily lives, we continually share snapshots of our social experiences with ever-expanding and overlapping circles of acquaintances. We ritualistically mark an occasion, such as a significant birthday, an anniversary, or a remembrance, by concentrating on stories that subtly and carefully bring to the fore an individual's vulnerabilities, passions, and idiosyncrasies. Like master storytellers of the past, we edit out the unnecessary infelicities and shine our light on the unforgettable characteristics and achievements we are witness to and, in the process, create yet another indelible substory, some of which may be told in years and even generations to come.

Prophets and preachers of all religions and creeds, too, have been masters of the practice and have relied on parables and maxims to communicate complex theologies to their followers. Parables of the tragedies of martyrs have drawn, and continue to draw, men and women to places of worship around the world, to shrines and town squares; such parables often comprise bits of truth side by side with bits of myth, using literary finesse to stir passions and breathe new life into common themes.

Those who hear or read these stories never seem to find the new variants of old themes tedious. Perhaps there is some reassurance in the predictability of how these tales of morality inevitably conclude. Modern-day films depicting the lives of greed merchants on Wall Street, spiced up with titillating subplots, are, in essence, adaptations of ancient lessons that one cannot serve both God and money. Furthermore, almost all morality tales ascertain that "lust for the flesh and the lust of the eye" invariably lead to trouble.

Hungry for stories that give us respite from the drudgery of our lives, we now gather before the pulpit of Instagram and Facebook and YouTube to get our daily fill of the antics of the modern deities, the 21st-century gods and goddesses and gurus who inhabit the heights of Hollywood and its tinseled replicas throughout the world.

For many communities and in many cultures, the most trustworthy narrators of irresistible tales are the poets. Poets, in their own inimitable ways, tell us about the challenges and failures of finding love and the joys of forming friendship. They warn us of the pitfalls, of the betrayals and injustices, that we always encounter along the way, yet encourage us to banish envy and the desire for revenge from our hearts. It is almost always the poets who teach us how to gauge the enormity of a loss, to grieve with dignity, and ultimately to accept mortality.

For more than eight hundred years, countless numbers of people in the Persian-speaking lands, and in recent decades many more around the world who have access to a growing number of excellent translations, have chosen Mowlana Jalal od-Din Balkhi, Rumi, as the spiritual teacher whose coruscating turn of phrase, coupled with the poignancy of candidly expressed emotion, has been a source of comfort as well as instruction.

Although the extent of academic scholarship on the philosophical and theological foundations of Rumi's order of mysticism now outweigh the poet's own writings, it is more rewarding to read Rumi's actual stories, which open the mystical portal to his world.

The stories that Rumi invents or reuses to aid in understanding the principles of Sufism are intricately woven into the warp and weft of the fabric of his teachings, yet to see them in isolation as the parables that they are, we need to painstakingly work our way through twenty-six thousand double lines of metrical verse, compiled in the six books of the *Masnavi-ye Manavi* (*Spiritual Couplets*), his magnum opus.

It is a relief and a delight to have the task completed for us by Maryam Mafi, one of the most respected, faithful, and eloquent translators of Rumi's poetry. Mafi the translator moves effortlessly between the two languages of Persian and English as she delivers the semantic meaning of the original text in English. However, Mafi the writer and close reader of the *Masnavi* transfers the exquisite subtleties, precise vision, and spontaneous wit of the original to the English version, thus giving life to Robert Frost's definition of poetry as "that which is lost out of verse in translation."

Mafi's own devotion to Rumi and years of study of his works alongside scholars of the field in Iran and elsewhere, as well as her impressive track record in translation, place her in a unique position to sustain "the afterlife" of the *Masnavi,* to borrow a phrase from Walter Benjamin in "The Task of the Translator." In her latest translation, *The Book of Rumi,* Mafi has turned her attention to more than one hundred stories that she has selected from the *Masnavi.* These stories include well-known and popular tales such as "Angel of Death," "Sufi and His Cheating Wife," "Moses and the Shepherd," "Chickpeas," and "Chinese and Greek Painters," as well as the less commonly quoted parables, "The Basket Weaver," "The Mud Eater," and "A Sackful of Pebbles."

The *Masnavi* of Mowlana Rumi offers numerous edifying epistles; it is an unmatched compilation of stories in verse that doubles as an elucidation of the philosophical and theological doctrine of Islamic worship. In page after page of parables and tales, Rumi not only entertains but also guides the reader, or more accurately the listener, in making sense of the complexities of life, in obeying the authority of love, and in resolving conflicts. Throughout the book, Rumi raises unanswered as well as unanswerable questions.

The cast of most of his tales are recognizable characters whose clones inhabit stories around the globe: wise or deceptive judges, cunning or distrustful women, wily or lachrymose beggars, charlatans, gullible souls, and many talkative animals. Rumi tells of kingly deeds and the miracles of prophets; he elaborates on the mischief of rouges and catches out mercenaries. Bodily functions, disguises, deeds of heroism, mistaken identities, sexual entanglements, consequence of gluttony and hubris, and all imaginative and extravagant accounts of vices and virtues, as well as common superstitions, are thrown into the mix.

The language of the poetic narrator of the tales soars to the heights of high verse with flawless use of metaphors and intricately structured internal dialogues, then plunges into the use of puns, vernacular idioms of the time, expressions of ribaldry, and pure bawdy humor. He quotes from the best of Persian and Arabic poetry of his era and relies on his scholarly knowledge of the Koran and the sayings of the Prophet Mohammed to support his arguments. Rumi is just as comfortable with the parlance of the lowlife and the rascals of the souk as he is with the rhetorical discourse of theologians at the mosque and grammarians at the madrassa.

Rumi deploys many dramatic devices to communicate with people from all walks of life. The roles that he assigns to animals, the flora and fauna, are in keeping with millennia-old traditions of storytelling in the East, where the sagacity of animals or their mischief-making are on par with human character.

No story is complete without a convincing and competent narrator, and the narrator par excellence of Rumi's stories whom we meet in the opening of Book One of the *Masnavi* is none other than the end-blown reed flute, whose breathy stories of separations, the pathos of exile, and the longing to be scorched by love immediately enrapture the listener. Thereafter, almost every page of the *Masnavi* contains a relevant or surprising story.

Mowlana Jalal od-Din, along with many of his medieval contemporaries in Iran, such as Sa'di of Shiraz and Nezami of Gandja, valued the potency of stories as the most reliable ambassadors to diffuse cultural and oral traditions across political, religious, and national boundaries.

If we were to conduct the most rudimentary survey of fables and old tales that exist around the world, we would realize quickly how closely they are linked; even fables told in far-flung lands, in languages that are endangered or only distantly related to the world's major languages, are often familiar, drawing comparison with tales we've heard since we were children. These fables not only travel from "breast to breast" and down through generations, they relocate across borders. Moreover, in the process of migration, bearing the hallmarks of their origins, they soak up many characteristics of the landscapes and societies at which they have arrived. Like the passport of a veteran traveler, the best and most enduring itinerant stories bear the stamp of each checkpoint at every cultural border crossing.

The most popular tales, whether from East Asia, the Indian subcontinent, Iran, or the Arab world, or those that originate in the heart of Europe, the Americas, or Africa, all share the same themes, motifs, and didactic tones, communicating the principles of morality and the values of courage and chivalry. It is therefore tempting to believe that all fables can be traced back to a single progenitor. Can we identify the original sources and locate them in a fixed time and a place?

Several scholars of Asian and Middle Eastern fables and folklore believe that the wellspring of legendary tales such as the *Thousand and One Nights*, the animal fables of *Kalila and Demna* that are reminiscent of *Aesop's Fables*, and the Persian wisdom tales of *Marzbānnāme*, is most likely none other than the *Jātaka*, a Pali collection of literature from India that dates back to at least 300 BC. The *Jātaka* tales recount the lessons and inner wisdom that spring from the many lives of the virtuous Buddha through his incarnations in human as well as animal forms.

The setting of the *Jātaka* tales is Banaras, or Varanasi as it is called today. This northern Indian city is known as the "Abode of Supreme Light" and the residence of the deity Shiva, the god of destruction and re-creation. Legend has it that Shiva dug the "well of wisdom" in that city, and its water continues to carry the "light of wisdom."

As these Indian stories began their journey west, they seem to have soaked up the colors of the wisdom/literature of the Parthians and Sasanians, and the attributes of their main characters seem to have been fused with those of the pre-Islamic Iranian legends, whose trials and tribulations inform much of the later heroic and romantic epics of the post–10th century Persianate world.

With the movement of people, the stories continued to wind their way further west and soon became infused with a body of lore from Arabic, Hebrew, Coptic, Greek, Syriac, Armenian, and Georgian oral and written traditions. The resultant hybrid interrelated fables have been told throughout these regions for well over a millennium.

It is in such a culturally rich but historically turbulent region in AD 1213 that we can locate a six-year-old boy by the name of Jalāl od-Din Mohammad, living in the city of Samarkand, now in Uzbekistan. Having moved from the outskirts of Balkh, Jalāl od-Din's family, headed by the patriarch scholar and cleric Bahāoddin Valad, had made Samarkand their home, a city described as one of the most prosperous and beautiful metropolises on the eastern edges of the Perso-Islamic empire.

A century earlier, the Persian medieval geographer, Istakhri, had depicted Samarkand and its surrounding districts as "the most fruitful of all the countries of Allah." Of the city itself, he wrote: "I know no quarter in it where if one ascends some elevated ground one does not see greenery and a pleasant place." Istakhri recounts that he once traveled out of the city for eight days through unbroken greenery and gardens, "where every town and settlement has a fortress . . . where the best trees and fruits are a plenty, in every home are gardens, cisterns, and flowing water."

Despite living and teaching in such paradisal surroundings, the forty-five-year-old Bahāoddin was anxiously contemplating the future of his family as

ominous political clouds were darkening the relatively peaceful horizons of Khorasan and threatening the tranquility of the diverse and multifaith city and its many centers of trade and learning. After all, Samarkand was the city that boasted the foundation of first paper mills of the Islamic world, in the middle of the 8th century.

The sense of foreboding was perhaps intensified by the unification a few years earlier of the Turko-Mongol nomadic tribes farther to the east under the leadership of Genghis Khan. How should have the inhabitants of Samarkand responded to the consolidation of Genghis Khan's power? Should they have feared him? Had he not sent emissaries to the ruler of this corner of the Persian empire with messages that sought neighborly trade? The accounts of the Persian historian Juvayni relate that Genghis Khan had greeted the Persian king in correspondence, saying: "I am the sovereign of the lands of the rising sun and thou the sovereign of the lands of setting sun. Let us conclude a firm treaty of friendship and peace."

Regardless of such assurances, the Valad family decided that remaining in Samarkand was not an option, and they left the region in 1216 and began an extraordinary journey that came to an end with their arrival in Konya in central Anatolia thirteen years later. During these thirteen years, the then nine-year-old Jalāl od-Din—who just over two decades later would be addressed by the honorific title Mowlana, "our master," and in centuries to come would be recognized across the world as Rumi, one of the most widely read and revered poets of all time—would travel a distance of more than seven thousand kilometers, meeting scholars, poets, spiritual teachers, princes, wayfarers, and a host of other characters who would appear in the pages of his *Masnavi* in due course.

After leaving Khorasan, the Valad family first made their way to the sprawling city of Baghdad, where no doubt the stalls of book dealers and bookbinders and sellers of inks and pens would have been a prime attraction. Perhaps it was in this city, divided by the sacred river Tigris, that a spiritual bond was forged across the centuries between Rumi and Mansur al-Hallāj, a mystical poet who had been gruesomely executed almost three hundred years earlier on the very same riverbanks.

It is said that while chanting "I am the Truth," Hallāj was beaten and lashed and hanged and decapitated on the order of the Abbasid caliph, and his remains were set alight on the shores of the river. Legend has it that as his ashes were thrown into the Tigris, the river foamed, and rose, and just when the startled onlookers thought that the city would be flooded, Hallāj's servant threw his now deceased master's robe onto the water, whereby the rapids were calmed, and the river was pacified.

According to Louis Massignon, a French scholar of Islam who died in 1962, a monument was built on the site of Hallāj's execution, but the structure was finally washed away in the Baghdad floods of 1921. Rumi, in his writing, often pays homage to the memory and teachings of Hallāj.

Taking their leave of Baghdad, Rumi's family continued their journey to Mecca, and after performing the hajj, set out for Damascus then on to Anatolia and the town of Malatya.

In Damascus, Jalāl od-Din would have walked the lanes of the gated city in the shadow of the ramparts dating back to Roman times. He would have strolled through the souk, where next to the vendors of sheep and birds and camel paraphernalia there would have been displays of spices, perfumes, and pearls, and glassware, pottery, and cinnabar in small shops. The young Rumi would have undoubtedly been taken to prayers at the Umayyad mosque and perhaps visited the Church of Mary. And all the while, whether consciously or by passive osmosis, he would have registered a host of plots and scenes that would gloss and nourish the body of stories that he would compose in verse before long.

It was during the family's travels through Syria and his father's meetings with fellow theologians that plans would have been made for Rumi to complete his studies by enrolling in the best madrassas and colleges of divinity, philosophy, and law in the cities of Damascus and Aleppo.

After spending a short time in the eastern Anatolian town of Malatya in the summer of 1217, the Valad family moved to Erzincan, and four years later to Laranda, the present-day Turkish city of Karaman. The Valads lived in this city until 1229. The young Jalāl od-Din was now a twenty-two-year-old married father of two small boys; the family had no doubt learned that the Mongols had invaded and destroyed the cities of Samarkand and Balkh. The torment of exile would have been compounded by this news of the near destruction of their homeland. A Persian eyewitness sums up the devastation wreaked by the Mongols on the city: "They came, they sapped, they burned, they slew, they plundered, and they departed."

After living in Karaman for seven years, Rumi, his elderly father, and the rest of the family set off once again, this time to Konya, a relatively short one hundred kilometers to the north. Konya became their final destination.

After the death of his father in 1231, Rumi returned to Aleppo to complete his studies before coming back to Konya and taking on his father's position as the head of the madrassa in 1237. Having excelled at academic studies, Rumi seemed to have been destined for an uneventful life of teaching his pupils, as he himself had been taught. However, his seismic encounter with Shams, the Sun of Tabriz, in November 1244 changed the course of Rumi's teachings and writings beyond the comprehension of most of his contemporaries.

The meeting between the thirty-seven-year-old erudite pupil of jurisprudence, Rumi, and the nearly sixty-year-old, often acerbic, peripatetic Sufi master, Shams, culminated in an intellectually and emotionally intimate friendship, which, although short lived, was a catalyst for the composition of some of the most beautiful lyrical odes and one of the longest single-authored narrative poems that has ever been written in any language. The six-volume *Masnavi,* in addition to his forty thousand ecstatic hymns to love collected under the title *Divan of Shams,* are Rumi's major works upon which rests his global reputation.

Rumi's voice in all his literary output, but particularly in the *Masnavi,* alternates between playful and authoritative, whether he's telling stories of ordinary lives or inviting the discerning reader to higher levels of introspection and attainment of transcendent values. Maryam Mafi's translations delicately reflect the nuances of Rumi's poetry while retaining the positive tone of all Rumi's writings, as well as the sense of suspense and drama that mark the essence of the *Masnavi.*

The Book of Rumi is another gem in Maryam Mafi's series of translations, which salutes the universality of Mowlana both as a poet and as a storyteller. I can think of no better tribute to the legacy of Rumi than Henry Wadsworth Longfellow's assessment of what makes a great poet:

> All that is best in the great poets of all countries is not what is national in them, but what is universal. Their roots are in their native soil; but their branches wave in the unpatriotic air, that speaks the same language unto men, and their leaves shine with the illimitable light that pervades all lands.

NARGUESS FARZAD

INTRODUCTION

Our essential need to gather together, paired with our compelling desire to share our experiences, thoughts, dreams, and entertainment, ultimately culminates in the act of storytelling. Stories are an ingrained part of lives everywhere, and in fact *life* is a series of successive stories with endless changing promises and surprises. Every experience in life embraces a backstory that may illumine and interpret the meaning of our lives. Like all skillful and worthwhile stories, ancient Sufi stories continue to be relevant to our lives today, because they're universal and timeless. The universality of a good story serves to demonstrate that we're not so different from our counterparts across the globe, which in turn prompts us to empathize with the "other" to the extent that we will eventually feel *as* the "other"; thus, respect and empathy are the inevitable by-products of this process.

Rumi's stories are a prime example of the perfectly timeless Sufi story, with a core message that is unvaried and that remains pertinent to us even in the mad rush of today's technologically driven world. Rumi's teaching stories are the core of his *Masnavi,* in which he raises commonsense issues that people grapple with regularly, but he concentrates on their hidden spiritual aspect, transforming them into profound Sufi lessons. In the *Masnavi,* Rumi includes many animal stories as well, mostly derived from other literary traditions, but he alters them somewhat to suit his purpose and prove his point.

We live in a fast age; everything moves more quickly—our cars drive faster, our appliances work more efficiently, we can access people across the globe on our mobiles for free, and of course we have the Internet, which itself transmits at ever increasing speeds. Living in rapidly evolving societies, where every minute counts and people never seem to have enough downtime, one can't expect that many people would choose to read long, unfamiliar, and perhaps tedious works of literature or commentary, regardless of how enriching or essential they may be.

By translating Rumi's works, I hope to reach out to people who may have never heard of him, especially the younger generation. But Rumi's longer, difficult, winding stories may not be the best introduction to his works, even though they contain deeply intense moral, psychological, and spiritual lessons that are well worth the attention of the dedicated reader. But Rumi wrote many short pieces that are equally complex and morally significant in their own way. Believing that these short works are more suitable as an introduction to Rumi and hoping that readers will be inspired to then seek out *all* of his works, including the longer pieces, I've decided to confine the present volume to Rumi's short stories.

I realized some years ago that every time I read a Rumi story, which he composed in verse, in my mind I instinctively turned it into prose as I was processing it. Throughout the years, many readers who are generally interested in spirituality but who are not great fans of poetry have expressed their disappointment in being unable to take full advantage of Rumi because of their lack of connection with poetry. With them in mind, as well as all Rumi lovers, I present this volume as a collection of Rumi's short stories translated into prose for broader accessibility.

Ritual has historically been an essential part of any society in which citizens come together to share meaningful experiences. Carrying out rituals that have connected people for millennia instills behaviors and thought patterns that shape the character of a people within their society. In Sufism, where ritual is taken extremely seriously, Sufis practice *zikr*, in which one or more of the ninety-nine names of God are repeated rhythmically for a certain length of time. The ritual is so profound that the practitioner can transcend beyond the present world and into the lap of God. It may not be possible for us today to attend *zikr* ceremonies regularly or at all, depending on where we live. We can, however, connect with the essence of *zikr* wherever we are.

I believe that connecting to Rumi on a regular, daily basis helps one, as in *zikr*, to transcend the interfering ego and lift one to a higher and purer

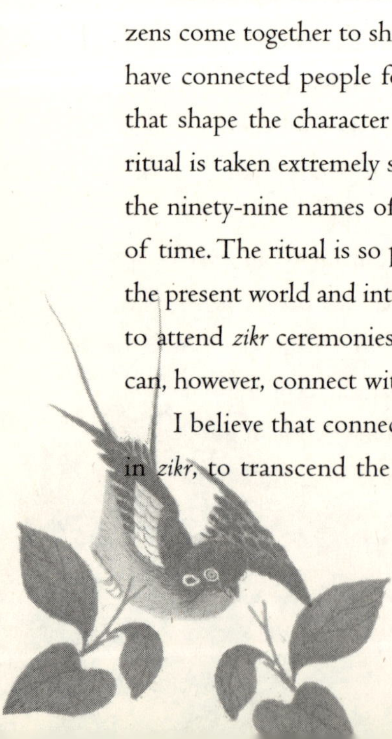

level of consciousness. I have personally made a ritual of reading a few verses of the *Masnavi* every morning before I begin my day to help me face the assault of the Internet and other modern-day forms of instant communication. If I can manage to practice yoga after reading from the *Masnavi*, I know that I will be guaranteed a serene and balanced mind and body to welcome the new day. The value of ritual, though, is in adhering to it, following it passionately, and not breaking the flow; this persistence in the practice of ritual is the greatest challenge. Reading one Rumi short story per day could easily become anyone's ritual.

To gather together a collection of stories that suits the taste of every reader is an impossible task. Yet in Rumi's stories, we come across such a vast and impressive spectrum of subjects, each with its unique appeal, that modern-day readers from diverse backgrounds and dissimilar walks of life are bound to find something of interest within. I'm confident that every reader will succeed in finding not one but many stories by Rumi to satisfy their curiosity for meaningful spiritual lessons, often sprinkled with sly humor.

MASNAVI I

The Parrot and the Grocer

There was once a grocer who owned a handsome green parrot who sang sublimely and spoke most eloquently. The parrot was not only an ideal companion but also the perfect guard for the grocer's shop. He kept watch all hours of the day and spoke amiably with the customers, entertaining them and thus increasing the grocer's sales.

One day when the grocer left the shop in the parrot's care, having gone home for lunch, a cat suddenly ran into the shop chasing a mouse, frightening the bird. As the parrot flew about in his effort to save himself, he knocked a few bottles of almond oil off the shelves, breaking them and covering himself and the shop floor in oil.

Not long afterward, the grocer returned and found the place in disarray, the floor slippery with oil and the parrot perching guiltily in a corner. In the wink of an eye, the grocer lost his temper and hit the bird on the head with all his might. The poor bird, who was already feeling guilty and downtrodden about his clumsiness, could not bear the shame, not to mention the pain from the blow, and he instantly shed all the feathers on his head.

Soon after the almond oil incident, the parrot completely stopped speaking and singing. The grocer realized how grave his mistake had been in striking the bird; not only had he lost his jolly companion but he had also curtailed his thriving business. Having no one but himself to blame, he now felt dumbfounded that he had singlehandedly threatened his very livelihood.

"I wish I'd broken my hand!" he lamented. "How could I have struck my sweet-voiced bird like that? How could I have behaved so monstrously?"

The grocer began to give alms to each and every poor darvish who passed by his shop, hoping that by doing good deeds he might be forgiven, and his bird might again start to exercise his mesmerizing voice. After three days and nights of remorse and suffering the parrot's silence, the grocer came into luck.

A bald darvish walked into the shop, and instantly the parrot began to speak: "Did you spill bottles of almond oil, too?"

The handful of customers in the shop were amused and smiled at the parrot, who had innocently thought that the bald man had suffered the same fate as himself!

"Darling little parrot," said one of the customers compassionately, "never equate one action with another. One must never compare oneself to others, even though they may appear to be the same on the surface; truly nothing is as it seems!"

The Angel of Death

Solomon, the wise prophet, held daily audiences during which he listened to his subjects' complaints and tried to address their problems. One morning, as he was listening to one person after another, a distraught man hurled himself into the great court. Solomon noticed how distressed the man was and beckoned him forward. Grateful for being invited to the front of the queue, the man fell to his knees before the great benefactor.

"What seems to be causing you such anguish, my dear fellow?" asked Solomon compassionately.

"The Angel of Death, my lord! I saw him a minute ago as I was crossing the street. He glared at me with such disdain that my heart nearly stopped!"

"We all know that Azrael takes his orders only from God and never wavers in his duties," asserted the great prophet. "Now tell me, what would you have me do?"

"I beg of you, my life's in your hands. Please tell the wind to carry me to India, where I'll be safe from the Angel's harm."

Promptly Solomon ordered the East Wind to carry the nearly paralyzed man to India and lay him down wherever he chose. He then duly returned to his other subjects' unattended affairs.

The following day when he returned to court, Solomon caught a glimpse of the Angel of Death among the crowd. He motioned the Angel to approach and asked him: "Why do you frighten people with that wrathful look, to the point that they abandon their livelihood and forsake their homes and family? What had that poor man done yesterday to deserve your crushing glare?"

Azrael was surprised. "My lord, I didn't look at him wrathfully at all! In fact, I was astonished to see him!" he said. "God had commanded me to take his pitiful life today in India, and I couldn't imagine, even if he had a million wings, how was he to get there on time. I was startled and gazed at him with surprise, not anger!"

When you look at everything in life with the eyes of want and greed, whom do you hope to escape? Yourself? God? Is that possible?

The Fly Who Thought She Was a Sailor

A poor donkey had been patiently carrying his heavy load all day long without a moment's respite. He had not even been allowed to stop to pee. Finally, his owner reached his destination, and the donkey was relieved of the merchandise heaped on his back. Free at last from his burden, the beast happily emptied his full bladder.

A short distance away, a tiny fly was resting on a leaf lying on the ground. The donkey's urine, flowing downstream, began to carry the leaf with the fly on it. The fly was initially taken aback, not quite understanding what was happening. After a little while, though, she began to believe: "I'm sailing away on the sea. I'm the captain of this ship, and what a perfectly seasoned navigator I am! Who dares to stop me now?"

The fly was gloating in her pride, floating on the stream of urine, believing that she was sailing the seven seas. Unbeknown to her, she was still the same lowly fly she'd always been, driven along by the furious pace of the urine's flow, unaware that nothing truly is as it seems.

Merchant and Parrot

Many years ago, a Persian merchant was given a beautiful parrot as a gift by his Indian trading partners. He kept the parrot in a formidable cage, where he could watch her and listen to her melodious song every day when he rested after his long hours at work. The time of year came when he normally traveled to India on a buying trip, and as is customary he asked his household help what they wanted him to bring back as gifts for them. Each person asked for something close to his or her heart, and so did the little green parrot.

"My dear master, my heart really desires nothing from my motherland," she said morosely. "But, should you come across a group of parrots like myself, would you please convey my greetings and tell them that I'm trapped in a cage in Persia, and I miss them terribly. Ask them whether they think it's fair that they're flying freely throughout the land while their cousin is slowly dying in captivity. I beg you to ask them on my behalf for advice on how I should reckon my situation."

The merchant didn't think much about the parrot's demand but promised to find the birds and deliver her message exactly as she had voiced it. Once in India, he diligently tended to his business but did not forget his promise of gifts for his servants or the parrot's message. One day, traveling from one town to the next, he happened to come across a group of parrots chirping noisily in a forest. He stopped his horse and delivered his parrot's message faithfully, but before he could finish, one of the parrots began to shiver uncontrollably, falling off the branch he'd been perched on and suddenly dying. The merchant ran to save the parrot, but the little bird looked perfectly dead!

He became distraught, feeling overwhelming guilt that he'd caused the poor bird's demise unnecessarily. He wondered whether the fallen bird was related to his parrot and had literally died from grief hearing about his trapped cousin. Was it not true that the human tongue is like an uneasy aggregation of rock and iron, which, when struck against each other, can spark off a fire? He regretted having recounted his parrot's message, but there was nothing he

could do now, so he continued with his duties until he finished them up, and then he returned home.

Upon his arrival, he distributed the gifts that each servant had asked for but said nothing to his parrot. The bird, who had been impatiently awaiting the response of her mates, grew increasingly impatient and at last couldn't hold back any longer, asking the merchant: "So, where's my gift? Tell me, what did you see and hear from the Indian parrots?"

"I'd rather not remember!" said the merchant somberly.

"Master, what's the matter? Why this long face?"

"I told your story to a group of parrots in the woods," he said reluctantly. "But, before I could finish, one of them began to shiver, then fell from the tree and died! I'll never forgive myself for causing the poor bird's death. But what's the use? Once the arrow has left the bow it will never return, and so are words that leave our lips."

But before the merchant could finish his sentence, the little parrot fell from her perch and dropped dead on the floor of the cage. The merchant could hardly believe his eyes; he burst into tears, quickly blaming himself for causing yet another innocent death. He became hysterical, cursing and repenting, not comprehending why all this was happening. He walked back and forth staring at his bird, who lay motionless on a heap of leaves on the floor of her exquisite cage. He caressed the parrot's feathers tenderly, remembering her harmonious song, which had given him so much pleasure for so long.

After a while, the merchant hesitantly opened the dainty cage door and carefully picked up the bird, carrying her to the garden and laying her on the ground while he dug a grave to bury her. Instantly, the parrot shot up to the nearest tree and perched on a high branch, looking contentedly at her former master. The merchant was awestruck, not fathoming the secret of the words he had uttered.

"My darling bird, I'm thrilled to see you're alive and well, but tell me, what did I say that prompted you to emulate your cousin in India? Tell me your secret now that you're free."

"That parrot was no relation to me, but by his action he taught me how to free myself!" confessed the jolly parrot. "Without actually speaking, he helped me understand that my imprisonment was due to my beautiful song, my talent for entertaining you and your guests. My precious voice was in fact the cause of my servitude! By his action, he taught me that my freedom would lie in the act of dying in the sense of forsaking my attachment to my worldly talents, which I had prized so highly."

The parrot bid her merchant master farewell for the last time and quickly flew out of sight.

The Old Harp Player

Gifted musicians were a great rarity in the old days, but it was during the reign of the famous Caliph Omar that a certain competent harp player earned himself a fine reputation. Spectators loved his voice, the melodious sound of his instrument, and his entertaining presence, and thus they paid him handsomely every time he played.

The years passed quickly; the musician aged, and his voice lost its sweet timbre. People no longer appreciated him, and the more he tried to sing, the more his voice sounded like the braying of a donkey. People would shoo him away, and by the time he turned seventy, he was impoverished and unemployable. Eventually he came to the end of his tether and at long last turned to God:

"My Allah, You've granted me a long life but I've been guilty! I never appreciated Your kindness, yet You never turned Your back on me and always provided me with my daily bread. But now, I'm old and feeble and no longer have a beautiful voice. In fact, my singing revolts people when not so long ago they couldn't get enough of it. I promise You that as of today I will only play and sing for You, my Beloved, and nobody else!" He sighed and, wishing for a little privacy, began to walk toward the town cemetery.

He found the graveyard empty as he walked silently, swerving between gravestones, until he finally chose a spot to sit down. Making himself as comfortable as possible, he began to play his harp to his heart's content until he was utterly exhausted and eventually fell asleep. He dreamed that he was in a lush meadow and that his soul's wings fully opened, carrying him lightly toward the sun. He wished from the bottom of his heart that he could stay floating in the air forever; but fate would not have it, as his time on earth was not yet up. At that very same moment, Caliph Omar, who was in his palace, uncharacteristically fell asleep in the middle of the day and had a dream in which God instructed him as follows:

"Omar, it's time to tend to my special subject! You can find him asleep among the gravestones. Take seven hundred dinars from the public funds that you collect on my behalf and take them to him as his wages. Tell him to come back to you for more after he's spent it."

Omar woke up with trepidation, grasping the urgency of his dream. He quickly ran to the graveyard and searched but could only find an old man asleep by a grave with an ancient harp by his side. At first, he wasn't convinced that this could be God's special subject, so he searched further but to no avail. At last he concluded that the harp player must be the man he was sent to find. Unwilling to disturb the old man, as he looked so peaceful, Omar quietly sat down beside him but then suddenly sneezed. The old man woke up with a fright and noticed the regal person sitting next to him. His heart in his mouth, he began to beg God to save him from what he thought was the Angel of Death.

Amused, Omar told him gently: "No need to fear me, dear one, I've brought you good tidings. In fact, Allah has greatly praised you and has asked me to pass on His blessings. He's also sent you seven hundred dinars for your overdue wages! When you've spent it, you're to come back to me for more."

The old musician couldn't believe his ears and became even more distraught than before. Agitated, he let out a heart-wrenching cry, tore off his tattered shirt, and, greatly addled, bit into his own hand. "One and only Allah, You've shamed me into nothingness!" he sobbed as he stood up and rambled aimlessly through the graveyard.

In due time, he stumbled back to find Omar and his harp still in the same spot as before. He picked up his precious instrument and, in one quick strike, shattered it against a nearby gravestone, destroying his only source of livelihood. "You've been the veil between God and me," he blamed the harp. "You're responsible for leading me astray from His altar. For almost seventy years, you've sucked my blood and made me shamefaced before my Creator," he said as he bashed the harp again and again, reducing it to insignificant slivers of wood.

"I beg Your forgiveness, my God," he continued. "I've sinned throughout this long life that You've gifted me. I've spent it singing and playing music, forgetting the pain of being separated from You, and I and no one else am the cause of my guilt and shame," he confessed. "Please save me from myself, for my enemy is within me, closer to me than my own pathetic soul!"

Omar comforted the agitated man, telling him that he must let go of his past as well as his future, for he was still entangled between them; and that meant that he was not yet one with God and had not yet put his full trust in the Creator. As he listened to Omar's wise words, the old musician felt a purer light rising in his heart, enveloping his body and soul. Astounded, he felt that he was letting go of the world he had known until then and found himself positioned in a different space, untouched by superficiality; a world that required an alternative understanding where no words were left to speak, where solitude and silence were the order of the day.

The Sailor and the Professor

It was late in the day, and the professor needed to cross the water to get back to the island where he lived. He jumped into the first boat he chanced upon and ordered the sailor to take him home as fast as he could. The boat slowly pulled away from the harbor, and the professor made himself comfortable on the deck. He took one long look at the sailor and decided that this man must be illiterate, and before he could control his tongue, he blurted out pompously: "Have you ever been to school or studied any literature?"

"No," said the sailor innocently.

"Then you've missed out on half of your life, my good man!"

The sailor was deeply insulted but didn't respond, carrying on with his work and waiting for an opportune moment to take his revenge.

Almost halfway through their journey, the weather turned, and a vicious storm kicked up. The sailor had finally chanced upon his moment of sweet revenge! Cunningly, he asked the professor, who was already white with fright: "Most revered master professor, do you know how to swim?"

"Don't be silly, of course not, my handsome and capable friend!" he stammered squeamishly.

"Oh, what a pity! Because now you're going to miss out on the rest of your life! The boat is caught up in a whirlpool, and the only way out is to swim! Now all your precious literature can't help you one bit. You thought me an idiot, and now look at you! Stuck in the mud like an ass!"

The Man Who Wanted a Tattoo

There is a town called Qazvin in central Persia where it was customary for wrestlers to tattoo parts of their bodies. One day, a man, who was not in fact a wrestler but who wished to pretend that he was brave and mighty, went to a tattoo artist who worked in the public bathhouse. He asked the artist to create a beautiful design on his arm that befitted his courage.

"What kind of design would you prefer?" asked the artist.

"A fierce lion, what else? My zodiac sign is the mighty Leo, so make sure you use the darkest blue you ever tattooed on anyone!" said the man arrogantly.

The tattoo artist took out his ink and pins and set to work. It only took a couple of piercings before the man couldn't bear the burning pain of the needle, and he snapped: "Which part of the lion are you tattooing?"

"I've started with the tail, sir."

"Leave it; leave the tail alone and start elsewhere," agonized the fake wrestler.

The artist went back to work, but as soon as he pierced the man's arm again the man began to scream in pain: "Which part are you painting now?"

"The lion's ear," reported the artist.

"Leave it; leave the ear alone and start elsewhere!" screeched the man, tears in his eyes.

The artist huffed and puffed but didn't say a word, going back to his work. Once again the fake wrestler began to scream: "What are you doing? Which part are you tattooing now?"

"The belly of the lion, sir," said the artist with disdain.

"Oh my God, this is unbelievable! Leave the belly alone, it's much too painful!" the man whined, unable to bear the burning pain. "Why should a beautiful lion need a belly at all?"

The tattoo artist was at his wit's end. Totally exasperated, he threw his tools to the ground and stepped away from his client.

"What kind of a lion tattoo doesn't have a tail, an ear, or a belly? God has not created such a lion!" he snapped. "Get out of my sight and don't ever dare show your face at my parlor again!"

Before the fake wrestler could even begin to complain, the tattoo artist grabbed him by the scruff of the neck and threw him out of the bathhouse into the cold winter air outside.

The Lion, the Wolf, and the Fox

A lion, a wolf, and a fox had become hunting partners. The lion was reluctant to be seen with the lowly fox and wolf but had yielded to their company because he thought it was his duty as the king of the prairie to allow them to benefit from his grace. Just as stars receive their light from the sun, the lion felt obliged to be magnanimous with respect to weaker and less worthy animals.

Their first hunt together in the high country was successful; under the lion's tutelage, the trio managed to capture a bull, a mountain goat, and a fat rabbit. With the lion's help, the two smaller animals carried their rich hunt from the mountain down to the prairie, their hunger growing by the minute. The wolf and the fox were too frightened to raise the issue of how the prey should be divided, but deep in their hearts they believed that the mighty lion would be fair in giving them their share; in fact, perhaps he would let them have most of the catch, as he was so magnanimous! The lion, for his part, could sense what his two companions were thinking, but he decided to remain quiet until an opportune moment arose when he would show them who was the decision maker among them.

"You lowly beasts, was my precious company not enough for you?" thought the lion to himself. "How dare you think that you can influence or predict my decisions? Don't you understand that every thought you have, every action you may take, are possible only because of me?"

While he entertained these thoughts, the lion erupted into laughter, prompting the wolf and the fox into thinking that soon they'd be filling their empty stomachs with their prey.

"Wolf," called out the lion. "Be my agent and divide the game. Be absolutely fair in your allocation. Show me what you're made of!" he challenged the wolf.

"My king, the big bull must be yours as it's the largest catch," declared the wolf, thinking he'd come to the best conclusion. "The mountain goat goes to me, as it's smaller and befits my size. The rabbit suffices the fox."

"You dare speak of *yourself* in my presence?" snapped the lion. "Fancying that you even exist while in the company of an unrivaled, majestic king is blasphemy! Come forward quickly," he ordered.

As soon as the wolf took his first step, the lion lifted his monstrous paw and ripped his head off, then shredded his body, leaving just a shell. "This low-born creature was entirely ruled by his ego! No room for him in my kingdom!" announced the lion nobly.

Once he was finished with the wolf, the lion turned to the fox. "Fox, it's your turn to divide the loot. Hurry up, as I'm feeling peckish."

The fox bowed respectfully, swallowing his fear. "Your honor, this fat bull is for your delightful breakfast," he said with nervous discomfort. "The mountain goat will be appropriate for your lunch, and the rabbit will suffice for your delectable supper."

"Where did you learn how to divide the loot in this manner?" asked the surprised lion king.

"From watching the desecrated body of the wolf, your honor."

"You're a smart fox," the lion admitted. "You've been absorbed into your love for me, and you've stopped regarding yourself as separate from the object of your love. Now you can only see me while you no longer exist; that's why I will let you have all three catches. Take them and be gone; I'll never hurt you. You may not only have the prey but I, too, am yours now! One who learns a lesson from watching his friends' mistakes is indeed the wisest one."

The fox couldn't believe his luck, silently giving thanks to God that the lion had first chosen the wolf to divide the loot; otherwise, it would have been his dead corpse sprawled over the prairie.

The Deaf Man and His Sick Neighbor

A man had been losing his hearing for some time but was too proud to admit his debility and continued to pretend that nothing was wrong with him. One day, a friend bumped into him outside his home and told him that the old man next door had taken ill and that it would be kind to pay him a visit, as he had no relatives to drop in on him. The nearly deaf man somehow made out what his friend was telling him and promised to visit his neighbor that very same day.

How was he going to approach his sick neighbor, wondered the deaf man, especially now that he had become ill and weak and likely able to speak only in a whisper? But there was no way out of it; custom decreed that he pay the old man a visit and inquire after his health. He decided that he'd decipher what the patient was saying by reading his lips and respond accordingly. Nevertheless, just to be on the safe side, he prearranged his questions in his mind and his neighbor's probable answers accordingly.

He decided that when he asked, "How are you feeling?" the sick neighbor would probably say, "Thanks be to Allah, I'm surviving." Then he'd say to him, "That's wonderful, thank goodness!" and continue: "What did you have to eat today?" The neighbor would probably reply, "I had a lovely vegetable soup, with a glass of cooling sherbet," to which he would respond: "Bon appétit; how wonderful!" In addition, he would ask: "Which doctor has prescribed your medication?" and the patient would probably tell him the name of one of the local doctors, to which he'd confirm, "Fantastic, he's the best in the trade."

Thus, he was encouraged by his plan and immediately went next door to pay his visit. He sat next to the old man's bedding, which was spread out on the floor, and kindly asked him: "How are you feeling, my dear neighbor?"

"I'm dying!" moaned the sick man.

"Thank God!" the deaf man said jovially, and continued with his next question, which he had duly prepared: "What did you eat last night?"

"Poison!" retorted the old man, already upset by the first answer.

"Bon appétit!" the deaf man responded obliviously.

The sick man, made even more upset by the last comment, bit his lips to stop himself from swearing at his annoying visitor. The deaf man, though, continued with his inquiries: "Which doctor is treating you?"

"Azrael, the Angel of Death!" snapped the sick man.

"May he be blessed. His presence is always good news; whomever he visits is cured of all his pains and aches forever!"

Unaware of the damage he had done to his sick neighbor's state of mind, the deaf man took his hand and shook it firmly before taking his leave, believing that he had done his neighborly duty and brought the sick man much joy and relief.

Chinese and Greek Painters

Chinese painters and their Greek counterparts in Asia Minor had been great rivals since the beginning of time, each considering themselves superior to the other. No one was truly able to say whose style was more sophisticated or which painters' works were more beautiful. This rivalry had gone on for much too long, and the sultan of Rûm, in Asia Minor, had become weary of the tireless backbiting on both sides.

Finally, he decided to stage a competition to establish once and for all which painters were the most accomplished and the worthiest of their time. The sultan decided to assign two of his empty cottages, which faced each other on the palace grounds, to the two groups of competing contestants. The Chinese were to occupy one cottage, while the Greek painters were to live and work in the one opposite. They had one month to present their projects to the sultan.

The Chinese were eager to begin work and asked for numerous colors of paint, immediately setting out to draw their designs on the walls of their house. The Greeks asked for nothing. They had brought with them special stones for polishing the surface of the walls. Shortly after arrival in their cottage, they began the grueling task of rubbing down the residue of many years of rot and decay that covered all the walls in their cottage.

It took the Greek painters countless hours of arduous work to remove the effects of many years of wear and tear on the aged walls, old paint and mildew that they scrubbed and polished over and over again. Meanwhile, their Chinese counterparts were busy applying layers and layers of paint, beautifying their own designs as they covered over what remained of the old paint.

The Greek painters were well aware of the art of the Chinese and were familiar with their methods. The Chinese, though, had no idea what the Greeks were up to. People were impatient to see what the great artists of their time had been working on and could hardly wait a day longer. After a month of labor, at last the artists were ready to show their masterpieces to the ultimate judge, the sultan.

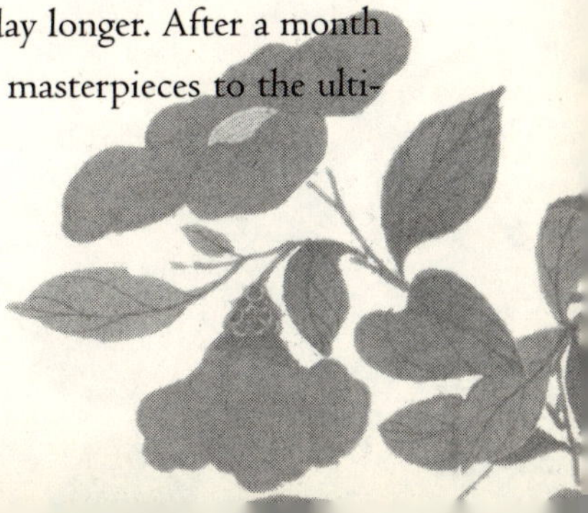

The judging day was upon them, and both groups of painters impatiently awaited the sultan's arrival. Musicians filled the palace grounds, and people danced and made merry while awaiting the final results to be called out. The sultan eventually arrived with his entourage and went directly to view the Chinese *chef-d'oeuvre*. The designs and the colors applied to the walls of the small cottage had transformed it into a grand palace of dreams! He had never seen such beautiful art in his life and was astounded. It took the sultan a very long time to detach himself from the beauty that surrounded him and to step outside the cottage.

Having seen what the greatest artists might possibly achieve, he was now exceptionally curious to see what the Greek painters had created. Reluctantly, he left the cottage of the Chinese painters and walked across to the other cottage, which was hidden from view by an enormous curtain. He ordered the curtain to be drawn back and instantly understood the miracle that the Greek painters had achieved.

Before the sultan stood the decrepit cottage, which in fact no longer seemed old or dilapidated. The mildew and stains of the past had been patiently and laboriously removed. The artists had scrubbed, polished, and refined the walls to the extent that everything, including the Chinese paintings in the cottage opposite, was perfectly reflected onto them, exemplifying their purity. The work of the Chinese painters, in all its complexity and beauty, was manifested in the art of the Greek painters' simplicity and transparency, thus rendering it unfathomably more glorious.

The sultan could not hide his amazement at how the Greek painters had managed to re-create beauty in its purest form, creating the perfect state. He had no doubt which group had the superior artists.

The Lover Who Was Nothing

A man, desperately in love, arrived at the house of his beloved and enthusiastically knocked on the door.

"Who's there?" asked the lady.

"It's me," declared the man, full of hope.

"Go away, there's no place for someone like you in this house!" she responded, her voice laced with sorrow. "You're naïve and not yet ready, just like an uncooked meal! You declare yourself as 'me' and still proclaim your undying love for *me*? A lover who only sees himself is no lover at all but needs to roast in the fire of separation until he's properly cooked!"

She refused to open the door, and the distraught man eventually backed away from the house. Soon after, he left the town for an unknown destination in some faraway land. Burning with the pain of separation, after a year of traveling from place to place he gathered his courage and approached his beloved's home once again. Apprehensively but politely, he knocked on the door.

"Who's knocking at this hour?" asked the lady impatiently.

"No one! The one on this side of the door is also you!" expressed the man humbly.

"Now that you've stopped seeing only yourself, you've become me at last! Two people could never exist in this house simultaneously, but now you may enter."

She cautiously opened the door and let her lover inside.

"Now you're welcome in this house. There's no difference between us anymore; no longer are we the rose and the thorn. We are one and the same."

Spitting at Imam Ali

In the early years of Islam in the Arab lands, the newly converted Moslems waged many wars with others who did not yet believe in Islam, people widely known as infidels. In one war, Ali, the prophet's son-in-law, who was a very competent warrior, came face to face with another capable soldier. Ali succeeded in bringing his opponent to his knees in a short, sharp fight and raised his sword to take the man's life. The proud soldier believed that his end was imminent, and all he could think to do was take one last spiteful action: he spat at Ali, right in the face. Ali immediately withdrew his sword and stepped back, sparing the man's life.

The subdued warrior was stunned; he had expected the worst and now was perplexed that he was still alive. He needed an explanation; he needed to know why Ali had taken pity on him. Before Ali could walk away from their encounter, the warrior called out to him: "Ali, you had drawn your sword to finish me off but changed your mind. What made you drop your weapon? What did you see in me when we fought that made you lose interest and spare my life? You had the upper hand; you'd won the fight. What else was more important than finishing me off? What suppressed your anger at that instant?"

"I only fight for God," responded Ali. "I'm God's servant; I'm not in the business of saving my own skin. I'm God's unbeatable lion, not a whimsical warrior of passion! Not words but actions speak for my belief. The sword might be in my hand, but it is God who strikes. Just like the wind that cannot move a mountain, I too shall not move other than by God's will.

"Anger makes most kings lose their heads, but anger is my obedient slave! It's indeed my patience that has freed me from the yoke of anger. My sword does not kill; instead, it bestows life! You spat at me, and thus raised an issue that did not directly involve God; and I never fight for any reason other than God. Your spitting aroused my ego and thus sparked off my anger. Had I used my sword, I would have been fighting half for God and half for my ego! That's why I thought it best to withdraw my sword."

Ali then turned to walk away, without looking back.

MASNAVI II

The Snake Catcher and the Thief

A petty thief was feeling supremely fortunate because, earlier that day, he had succeeded in stealing a massive snake from a snake catcher. Little did the witless thief know that it had been the snake catcher's first catch, and even less was he aware that the snake's venom was deadly! Meanwhile, the snake catcher was himself oblivious to his luck in losing the snake, of whose danger he was himself unaware. Distraught at his loss, though, he schemed about how to find the thief and retrieve his precious catch, which he had hoped would fetch him a tidy sum.

Not long afterward, the snake catcher was making his way into town, toying with various plans to catch the thief. All of a sudden, he saw the thief's dead body by the roadside and recognized him instantly.

"It must have been my snake that took his life!" the snake catcher gasped as he spotted the tracks the snake had left by the side of the corpse as it wiggled away. "I prayed so hard to find this poor soul and get my catch back, believing I'd been cheated. Praise to God that my prayers went unheeded. While I thought I had lost a salable snake, in fact I had gained back my life!"

Many are our wishes and prayers that, beyond our ability to see, will only bring us loss or death, which God Almighty turns a deaf ear to simply out of His benevolence.

Jesus and the Skeleton

Jesus often traveled from place to place, and various people tended to accompany him for parts of his journey. On one occasion, as he was leaving a small village, a young man began to follow him. Not long after they had set out, the young man spotted the bones of some anonymous creature in a ditch. His curiosity was raised, and, believing that he had discovered an abandoned human skeleton, he started to poke the bones with his stick.

"Are you not the greatest prophet on the face of the earth?" he asked Jesus. "Then you must know the secret of bringing back the dead!"

Jesus ignored his comment, but the man persisted: "Please, great prophet, teach me how to give life to these useless bones, so that I too can say that I've accomplished a worthy deed."

Jesus was annoyed and continued to ignore the young imbecile, but the man wouldn't relent and repeated his request again and again. Jesus was beginning to lose patience, and, sure enough, he eventually snapped: "Be quiet, this is no task for a fool! This work requires a soul purer than rainwater, a self more sentient than angels. You must live many holy lives before you can even be considered a candidate for such a job. Let's just imagine for argument's sake that you found a suitable staff, but where now is Moses to achieve the miracle?" Jesus tried his best to make the simpleton grasp the importance of the issue.

"All right, since you think that I'm not good enough to know the secret prayer, then *you* do it. *You* give these bones life!" he repeated unrelentingly.

Utterly puzzled, Jesus wondered why this apparently ego-ridden man was so bent on bringing these dead, forsaken bones back to life. He turned to God, imploring Him to divulge the reason for this challenge, and soon he heard a voice in his head:

"The piteous always drive themselves into a rueful state. They plant seeds but sow thorns. And those who sow thorns have no place in the divine Garden. In their hands, every rose will become a thorn. If they fall in love, their beloved will turn into a venomous snake, for their spirit is dark and nasty. Their talent is in creating poison, unlike the true alchemist, who turns everything into precious gold!"

Quite curious by now, Jesus decided to fulfill the young man's demand, hoping to discover the purpose of this predicament that he found himself in as well as ridding himself of the fellow's exasperating company. Thus, he uttered the prayer to raise the dead and blew it onto the shattered bones.

Unbeknown to Jesus and the young half-wit, the bones were not those of a man but of a fierce black lion. In no time, the lion, raised from the dead, snapped the young man's head off, broke his arms and legs, and shredded his body. Standing a few paces away, Jesus witnessed the attack in awe. Cautiously, he approached the lion: "Why did you tear this poor man apart? He just made me give you back your life!"

"I decimated his body because he had made you angry, O great prophet!" said the lion obediently.

"Then why don't you eat his flesh?" inquired Jesus.

"It's not my fate today to be nourished by his body!" replied the grateful lion, who then turned around and walked toward the distance.

The King's Falcon

The king had a deep love for falcons and was indeed an accomplished falconer. He kept a separate area of his palace dedicated to his outstanding birds and visited them regularly. One afternoon, after he'd finished some routine business with his advisers, he decided that it was the perfect time to fly his favorite falcon. But, alas, when he entered the enclosure he saw that the bird had escaped!

The falcon, having been reared in the palace all her life and cared for tenderly by the king himself, had somehow gotten out and lost her way, and had ended up at an old woman's cottage. The woman was preparing a pot of soup for her family when she caught sight of the astounding bird perched on her wall. She felt sorry for her and grabbed her by the talons, tying them up with a piece of string so she couldn't fly away, and began to stroke her beautiful feathers.

She decided, though, that the bird's long, unkempt feathers needed pruning, so she cut them as short as she thought appropriate. Then she noticed the bird's talons and thought it best to cut them as well, for they seemed not to have been trimmed for a long while. The entire time she tended to the poor falcon, she stroked her caringly and whispered to her sympathetically: "Where have you been, little one, that they've treated you so badly? Look how long your feathers and nails had grown! You should've flown to Mother much sooner."

The lost falcon was now trapped for good, unable to fly or climb away. Meanwhile, the king and his soldiers had searched the entire county for her and were returning to the palace empty-handed and downhearted. As they rode through the last village on their route, all of a sudden, the king caught sight of his poor falcon, who didn't look anything like her old, beautiful self but was still completely familiar to the king. In the midst of the smoke and dust of the old woman's poor hut, the bird had lost her glory; the glamour of the palace had been completely washed away.

Tears welled up in the king's eyes, and he spoke: "This is your punishment for being ungrateful and forsaking my blessing. Ending up in this

disgusting hut with this old, ignorant woman is what you truly deserve!" The king reproached his bird while stroking her injured feathers lovingly.

The falcon was shamefaced and looked at her master with utter surrender and regret. If only she could speak, she would tell the king how sorry she was for being so naïve and ungrateful. Without words, she begged the king for forgiveness, admitting that she had taken her noble stature for granted.

With her expressive eyes, she confessed that even though she'd lost her feathers and talons, she was not unduly distressed because they would eventually grow back; she implored that she would gladly tolerate the pain of her diminished grandeur in the meantime, because she knew that the king was a merciful master! If only the king could find it in his heart to forgive her transgression, just this once!

The Shaykh and the Tray of Sweets

There was once a famous shaykh who was revered by everyone in the small town where he lived, but he was always in debt. Renowned for his generosity and selflessness, he gave away to the poor everything that he was given by the rich. With the last donation he had received from a wealthy patron, he built a Sufi House, leaving himself with nothing to spare. He remained untroubled, though, as his debts had always been paid through the grace of God—until then! His life's end was approaching, and he lay in bed contentedly, melting away like a candle, while his creditors gathered around him, sour faced and desperate, as they had no hope of collecting what was owed to them.

"Look at these untrusting fellows!" he thought as he watched them from his sickbed. "How could they not trust that God will repay my measly debt?"

In a trice, he heard a child's voice outside selling sweet halva. The shaykh ordered his manservant to purchase the entire tray, hoping that perhaps when the angry creditors ate something sweet they would not glare at him with such bitterness and disdain. The servant bargained with the child and bought the whole tray for half a dinar, setting it down before the men. The shaykh graciously invited them to enjoy it. When the tray was polished clean, the boy asked for his money.

"How do you expect me to pay you?" the shaykh retorted. "I'm on my deathbed; go away, leave me in peace!"

Frustrated and overcome with grief at his loss, the boy hurled the empty tray onto the floor, wailing uncontrollably. He cried out, wishing that his legs had been broken or that instead he had gone to sell his sweets at the bathhouse rather than at this wretched Sufi House with its freeloading mystics. A crowd gathered around the boy as his sobs echoed throughout the neighborhood: "Great shaykh, I assure you that my master will murder me on the spot if I return empty-handed. How can your conscience permit this injustice?" he pleaded with the shaykh as he stumbled up to his side.

"What are you conjuring?" protested the creditors at the dying shaykh. "You've already usurped our wealth. How could you now bring such misfortune upon this poor lad?"

Impervious to the men's retorts and pretending to be unaffected by the weeping boy, the shaykh pulled his quilt over his head and slept soundly. The boy remained beside him, weeping until the next prayer time, and the shaykh did not glance at him once.

Why would the full moon, in all its glory, be bothered by the barking of moonstruck dogs? Does the moon even hear their noise? The beasts do their job while the moon does its own, spreading light all over the world. All things on earth and above do their own little task; running water does not lose its clarity or calm because of the straw and dust that float on its surface! The king, amused by his entertainers, drinks his wine by the stream until dawn, unaware of the cacophony of the frogs around.

Had the creditors collectively dug into their pockets to gather the half dinar that the shaykh owed the boy, they could have easily paid him off. Yet the will of the shaykh prevented them from exercising their generosity and the boy from receiving anything at all. Such, and much more, is the power and mystery of a Sufi.

At the next prayer time, a servant arrived with a covered tray sent by one of the shaykh's wealthy admirers who knew that he was unwell and didn't have much longer to live. The servant paid his respects and laid the tray before the shaykh, lifting the cover to expose a small banquet of exquisite sweets. Much to everyone's surprise, there lay four hundred dinars in a corner of the tray and half a dinar separately wrapped in a cloth by their side. The creditors gasped in awe, unable to fathom how the shaykh had managed to bring about such a miracle. Instantly they repented, ashamed to have ever doubted his powers, and begged his forgiveness.

"I forgive you all your doubts," the shaykh replied. "Go in peace. I asked God to show me the right way, and thus He did! Although this half dinar is not worth much, to gain it depended on the tears of the child! Unless the sweet-seller boy cried his heart out, the doors of benevolence would not be flung open. My brothers, by the child I mean the child in your own eyes! Consider your needs fulfilled once you shed tears. If you want to be the recipient

of unbounded generosity, make the child in your eyes cry for your earthly body."

We cannot judge the behavior of mystics with our simple minds. Unless we suffer occasionally and express our hopelessness, the doors of grace cannot be opened to us; as in this case, the boy's tears were required before the gates of generosity could be unlatched.

The Sufi Who Lost His Donkey

A merchant darvish would travel for several days in a row, trading his goods in towns and villages that he passed through. One night after a long journey, he arrived at a remote town on the edge of the desert. As was customary for darvishes, he sought the nearest Sufi House to spend the night. When he located the establishment, he went directly to the stables to tend to his exhausted donkey, who had patiently carried the merchandise all day. He brought him plenty of water and hay, making sure that the animal lacked nothing for want. Just to be sure of his donkey's well-being, he tipped the young stableboy to take extra care of him.

The other darvishes who were staying in the Sufi House were mostly poor and hungry laborers, their hearts habitually on the verge of sin. When they realized that the newcomer had a donkey in the stables, they decided to take advantage of their sudden fortune. Unbeknown to the owner, they quickly sold the donkey to another guest who was leaving that very same night and spent the money buying food and candles for the evening.

As they began to prepare their meal, the men became progressively more agitated, excited that tonight everything was perfectly set for a grand feast. They extended much courtesy to the donkey's owner, bowing to him repeatedly and making him feel welcome. Meanwhile, among themselves, they silently celebrated the fact that they no longer needed to beg for a morsel of food, nor would they have to fast for lack of resources in the coming days. The owner, for his part, considered himself lucky to be at the Sufi House that evening and able to enjoy a tasty meal in the company of great, generous Sufis. Little did he know!

Eventually, the food was served, and all enjoyed themselves, eating to their hearts' delight. Soon after they finished their meal, the men began the *sama.*[1] The dust rose under their feet, mingling with the smoke from the cooking,

1. Spiritual whirling dance of Sufis.

enveloping the whirlers in a mystic cloud. The Sufis sang and danced, raising their arms toward the sky, whirling round and round, stomping their feet then prostrating on the floor, sweeping it clean with their robes. As the *sama* gathered pace, the musicians picked up the beat and began to sing enthusiastically: "The ass is gone, the ass is gone!"

Arms in the air, the *samazans*[2] repeated madly after the musicians: "The ass is gone, the ass is gone!"

The owner of the donkey, unaware that it was *his* donkey they were singing about, joined in passionately and sang along with them: "The ass is gone, the ass is gone!"

The *sama* continued long into the night, lasting until dawn. At sunrise, the men left one by one on their separate ways, bidding each other warm farewells. The owner of the donkey wiped the dust off his clothes and gathered his belongings, getting ready for another working day. Hurrying to catch up with his newfound darvish friends, he rushed to the stables but did not see his four-legged companion. He thought that the stableboy must have taken the animal to the stream to let him drink; perhaps he hadn't had enough water the night before. When the young boy finally appeared, the owner asked him about his donkey's whereabouts. The boy was confounded and told him that he had no idea what he was talking about. The owner became furious and grabbed him by the throat, threatening him with his life.

"I left my donkey in your care last night," he screamed. "You were meant to look after him. Don't you dare give me excuses; quickly go and bring him to me—otherwise, I shall take you directly to the authorities!" he threatened.

"I was overpowered by the darvishes," confessed the boy. "I feared for my life! They sold your donkey and used the money to purchase the feast last night. To leave a loaf of bread with a group of hungry men is like throwing a scrawny cat to a pack of wild dogs!" he exclaimed, trying to view the situation philosophically.

"Supposing they took him from you by force, shouldn't you have informed me that they were stealing my donkey? If you had, I could have at least bought

2 Sufi whirlers.

him back from the buyer or got the money out of this unruly lot. Now that they've each gone their separate ways, how am I ever going to find them? What an irreparable injustice you've brought upon me!" he whimpered.

"I tried to warn you several times, I swear to God, but your enthusiasm was greater than all of theirs put together!" retorted the stableboy. "You sang even louder than the rest: 'The ass is gone, the ass is gone!' I thought for sure you must have given them your consent, being a mystic and privy to so many secrets!"

"I was excited, aroused by their enthusiasm," agreed the darvish. "But I was foolish to imitate them. Imitation has destroyed me! I curse it a thousand times, for it has damaged me beyond repair!"

The Man Who Killed His Mother

In one of the poor neighborhoods of town, a woman had been sleeping with every man who approached her. One day, her son, who could no longer bear the shame, stormed into her bedroom. He attacked her with his dagger, stabbing her repeatedly, making sure that she was dead.

His will was resolute, and he kept his head up as he staggered out of the house, his clothes stained with her blood. He walked purposelessly along the back streets of the neighborhood for several hours until a friend chanced upon him and soon heard his confession.

"But, my friend, why did you kill *her*? I don't understand," the friend asked him, completely perplexed.

"She was a prostitute and shamed me every day!" blurted out the young man, angry that his friend had not understood his pure intention and was now questioning him.

"Why didn't you kill her *lovers*? Why kill *her*?" repeated the confused friend.

"I would've had to kill a man a day!" rationalized the troubled man. "This way her shame is buried with her for all time, and I don't ever have to commit another murder."

Sound of the Splash

It had taken the villagers a long time and had cost them a fortune, but they reasoned that it had been necessary to build a wall to protect their water supply from possible theft by their neighbors in the next village. One hot summer day, a man was passing through the area, but his thirst overwhelmed him. As he staggered slowly along the wall, taking advantage of the little shade it provided, he hoped to find a way to the stream to sate his thirst.

The sound of the running water was unmistakable, and soon the poor, thirsty man was unable to take another step. He spent his last remaining strength to climb the wall to at least catch a glimpse of the running water on the other side. When he reached the top, he instinctively scooped up a handful of mud from the wall and tossed it into the stream. The sound of the splash was music to his ears, and his heart was lifted out of its desperate gloom. He was thus encouraged to continue scooping out more mud and chucking it into the water, just to hear the melodious sound of the splash. As he listened to the music of the water, a question arose in his mind: "What do you hope to achieve by throwing mud into the stream?"

"For a thirsty man, the sound of the splash is like the music that raises the dead on Judgment Day!" he replied to no one in particular. "It also reminds me of the sound of thunder, which announces the arrival of rain to a scorched garden; or the gracefulness of alms to the darvish; or even a prisoner's hope for freedom."

Almost forgetting his thirst, the man continued to flip mud into the stream, enjoying the enchanting sound of the splash.

"Oh, and there's something else that's just as important!" he seemed to remember. "I'm no engineer, but I can see that with every handful that I dig, the wall gets lower, allowing *me* to get closer to the water! Slowly but surely, this tall, sturdy wall is going down, and in no time, I'll be only a stone's throw away from the object of my desire, namely that stream of fresh, running water, which is my life!"

Thorny Shrubs

In the past, desert towns and villages were connected by long and circuitous dirt roads. In one such village, there lived a vicious man who cared for no one, not even for his immediate family. He seemed to be always in conflict, mostly with himself; one could gauge his mood simply by watching whether he was involved in some vindictive activity.

For some time, this man had been planting small, thorny shrubs along the road from his village to the next. These bushes grew slowly but sturdily and scratched against the feet and legs of whoever walked on the path, turning their journey into absolute torture. Every day, he planted new shrubs despite the complaints of other townsfolk; he offhandedly turned a deaf ear to the village headman's order to stop his spiteful planting.

Although he regularly promised to pull out the thornbushes, he never complied, and they grew sturdier and thicker, cutting the skin of people using the footpath and causing bleeding infections. At last, the selfish man was called to court.

"I've asked you many times to stop your unreasonable planting," gushed the headman. "Why do you insist on hurting everyone around you? Every day you break your promise to pull out the thornbushes, you lazy good-for-nothing! I've ordered you to pull out the nasty plants but instead you leave them to grow, further strengthening their roots; and you add more every single day! You grow older and weaker each day as they grow stronger and taller. Either you cut them from the roots this very morning or turn them all into rose bushes! Tell me, can you do that?"

The headman had legally challenged the scofflaw at last, but he didn't have much hope, nearly certain that his words would have little impact. He knew that it was probably too late for this damaged soul to change his deeply ingrained ways, and he watched the man in despair as he left the courtroom in a careless clamor, plainly indicating with his disregard that he had no intention of heeding the court order.

Zolnoun in the Hospital

The great Egyptian Sufi Zolnoun had apparently gone insane. His unbounded excitability had become disturbing to everyone close to him. Yet his devotees were tolerant and put up with his increasingly unbearable behavior, until it reached a point that he truly became quite insufferable. When his fiery madness became contagious and affected the behavior of the citizens he regularly came across, it became evident to his friends and devotees that Zolnoun had to be admitted to a sanatorium.

Although, truthfully, the great Sufi could have easily controlled and repressed his impulsive behavior and avoided being taken forcefully to a prison-like hospital, he refused to submit to the will of those around him, who simply did not possess his depth of insight. Zolnoun, who had literally been driven to insanity by the sheer number of people who surrounded him at all times, was in fact thrilled to find peace and quiet at last in the hospital. He spent his days silently reading and studying his favorite texts, happy to be left to his own devices. However, his peaceful state did not last long, and soon those of his followers who considered themselves his close friends and companions could not bear his absence any longer and decided to pay him a visit.

Zolnoun was sitting peacefully in the garden of the sanatorium reading when he saw these men he knew approaching. In the blink of an eye, the calm and composed Zolnoun of the past weeks was transformed into a screaming and cursing madman. His friends were not at first too concerned, as they believed they'd already seen him in this insane state and thought nothing of it.

The old Sufi, however, noticed that his usual ranting was no longer working and decided to test his so-called friends even further. He began to run around the garden spitting and cursing, gathering up rocks and sticks and hurling them at the men. At first they thought that this frantic behavior could not continue for long, but they soon discovered that Zolnoun, although feeble looking, was indeed stronger and more energetic than even they, who were still young men.

It didn't take long for Zolnoun to achieve his purpose, which was ultimately to scare the men and drive them off the grounds of the sanatorium. He laughed out loud as he watched the men hurry to save themselves from the projectiles he'd thrown at them. Waving his arms frantically about him, he screamed after them: "I spit on you and your so-called friendship! A true friend tolerates any kind of behavior; he doesn't give up on you after only a few foul words and some stone throwing! How could anyone consider the likes of you to be friends? Be gone and good riddance to you all!"

Once alone again, Zolnoun sat quietly on his favorite bench in the garden of the sanatorium, reading his favorite treatises on friendship.

Loghman and His Master

In ancient times, wealthy people owned slaves, and Loghman belonged to a kind and loving master. The master had witnessed his devoted slave perform his duties without fail and with total honesty and loyalty through the years. He was as devoted to Loghman as the slave was devoted to him, to such an extent that the master thought he might even love his slave more than his own children.

Although Loghman was only a slave, he had many qualities of a highly spiritual person. His master was so fond of him that he refused to touch any food before allowing Loghman to taste it first. If the slave didn't eat what was offered to him, the master would throw the food away without touching it. One day, an acquaintance brought a gift of rare melons from his farm. It was the end of the summer but still hot, and Loghman decided to submerge a couple of the melons in a shallow pool to cool them before serving them to his master that afternoon.

The day had cooled down a little, and the master had awoken from his afternoon nap when Loghman quickly brought the cool melons for his delight. The master chose a long knife and cut a thin slice of the fruit, but as usual before tasting it he first offered it to his favorite slave. Loghman took the melon and gratefully bit into it, and in no time he finished it delectably. When the master saw how much he had enjoyed the first slice, he cut him another. Loghman ate the second slice with such craving that his master continued to give him more and more. Finally, there was only one last slice left, and the master thought he'd better taste it himself.

With great pleasure, the master took a bite of the delicious-looking melon, but before he could even begin to chew his mouth was on fire! The melon was so bitter that the master's mouth was immediately covered in blisters such that he could hardly breathe. It took over an hour for him to regain his composure and speak: "My dear man, how could you eat the entire melon, which was as bitter as poison, and smile at me with such joy in

your eyes? Are you your own worst enemy?" he asked with great compassion in his words.

"My revered master, all my life you've fed me the most delectable foods. I was too ashamed to complain, as it was the first time that you'd given me something unpalatable. The reason for my whole existence is your benevolence; how could I possibly complain about one instance of being served inedible food?"

Moses and the Shepherd

It was almost sundown, and the heat of the day was abating. The shepherd had gathered his herd of goats and was heading home. A soft, cool breeze had begun to blow, making the thought of the imminent night even more delicious. The shepherd was in a good mood and was lovingly praising his beloved God, unaware that the prophet Moses was within earshot:

"Where are You, my one and only Beloved, so that I may serve You without fail, mend Your shoes when they're torn, comb Your locks when they're untidy, wash Your clothes when they're soiled, and pick the lice out of Your disheveled hair? My magnificent Beloved, I promise to always kiss Your hands with utter respect, bring You fresh milk every day, and rub Your tired feet when they're painfully sore. When it's time to sleep, I'll make Your bed and sweep Your room spotless. My life's Yours to do with as You wish; my goats, my entire livelihood, all belong to You, for You're my one and only Love."

Moses patiently listened to the shepherd's blasphemous litany until he finally fell silent. Gravely he stepped forward and asked the simple shepherd with authority: "Who were you speaking to?"

"The One who created you and me, the earth and the sky," replied the shepherd innocently, not recognizing Moses.

Moses could not hold back his anger and exclaimed in horror: "You miserable, pitiful man! What's this nonsense you're spitting out? I'm Moses, your prophet, and I'm telling you to shut your disdainful mouth this instant. The Creator has no worldly limbs; shoes are for those who need them, milk is for someone who's still growing! Your praise makes no sense, so stop it before your life is forever cursed!"

Astounded and ashamed, the shepherd sighed: "Oh, Moses, you've sewn my lips together! I repent and wish that my life could be set on eternal fire this very minute!"

He then stood up, ripped open his shirt, threw it to the wind, and sobbed desperately into the desert. Soon after this encounter, Moses felt a heavy

slumber descend upon him, sending him into a deep sleep, where he had a revelation:

"Moses, what have you done?" Moses immediately recognized the undeniable sound of God's voice. "You've alienated my faithful servant from me! Did I send you as my prophet to unite me with my people or to sever me from them? I've allowed everyone their own way of worshipping, their own form of expression. I have no need of their prayers, but *they* do. What may seem like poison to you could be honey to someone else. I don't look at what my people say outwardly, I only see what's inside their hearts. I want to see the burning of love! So light up the fire of love in your soul and banish your unhelpful thoughts once and for all!"

Hearing God's words, the treacle of His wisdom was implanted in Moses's soul, opening his eyes to secrets unknown to him before and convincing him to always look beyond the superficial. A few moments later, he was heading into the desert on the trail of the shepherd, agonizing over his harsh and unkind words to the poor man. It didn't take long to find the shepherd's footsteps, for they were distinctly different from an ordinary man's. In places he'd been dragging his feet, and soon after that he'd been limping, then sidestepping and stepping backward, even crawling at times, all indicative of his tumultuous state of mind. In due time, Moses spotted the shepherd in the distance and carefully approached him, speaking softly:

"My dear shepherd, you've been blessed by God Almighty himself! He has reproached me for speaking to you so abrasively. He wants you to pray in any way you prefer. In fact, God adores your simple words that come directly from your heart. You may continue in the same manner that you've always prayed, and God wants you to know that He's absolutely content with you."

The shepherd raised his face to Moses. He was not the same man anymore; his eyes did not belong to this world, and his voice rose from a more profound depth.

"Moses, I've gone beyond your hollow words; I'm mad in my soul. I've traveled past the earth and the sky, a thousand years beyond! You brought down your whip on my very being, hurling me into worlds beyond my dreams. Praise be to your whipping arm, which laid such a blow and roused me to my own truth. I can't explain who or what I am anymore; all I know is that I'm sailing away, but where to, I cannot tell."

The shepherd said goodbye respectfully, turned his back to Moses, and staggered away, traveling deeper into the desert until he became invisible.

Friendship with a Bear

The mountains in the northern part of Persia were rampant with large brown bears who roamed the vast region and hardly ever had to defend themselves against any predators. There was, however, one extraordinary beast that the locals had never set eyes upon called a dragon, which could easily kill and devour the bears.

A hunter from the central part of the country went to the mountains in the north in search of prey, but he knew nothing about the legendary dragon. As he pitched his tent and prepared a fire to keep himself warm overnight, he hummed his favorite melody, excited about his anticipated morning hunt. All of a sudden, he heard the excruciating cry of a beast and the piercing roar of some other creature that he had never heard before. His curiosity was aroused, and he picked up his bow and arrow and swiftly but carefully approached the scene of the fight.

Right there before him was the elusive dragon with fire coming out of his mouth as he flashed his huge sharp teeth at an enormous bear, the latter standing on his hind legs preparing for the imminent fight. The hunter wasted no time, aiming straight between the dragon's eyes and shooting him on the spot. Down fell the dragon with the most hideous sound thundering from his fiery mouth. The bear, looking upon the scene in disbelief, was stunned. He turned to the hunter and gazed at him for a while before lowering himself onto all fours and slowly swaggering over to him.

At first, the hunter was alarmed that the bear might attack him, but his fears were eased as the huge animal sat before his savior's feet, resting his head on his paws. It seemed to the hunter that the animal was demonstrating gratitude in his own way, and he was relieved. As he turned around to walk back to his tent, the bear got up and quietly began to follow him.

From that day on, the bear never left the hunter's side, and the hunter gradually became accustomed to his presence. The two became odd companions, much to the surprise of everyone who saw them together. Often, people would warn the hunter that to befriend an ignorant beast was dangerous, even worse than making friends with a human enemy. The hunter, though, never heeded their advice, believing that his advisers were all jealous of his friendship with the glorious bear. Soon, everyone stopped giving him advice, leaving the hunter to his own devices.

One glorious morning, the huntsman decided to take advantage of the good weather and go hunting. The two companions traversed a variety of mountain paths in search of a worthy prey, but they were unlucky and still empty-handed after many hours of aimless pursuit. The hunter grew weary and decided to take a short nap in the shade of a tree. The bear had learned to obediently sit by his side and guard him and his bow and arrows until he awoke.

As the hunter slept deeply, dreaming of beautiful long summer days, a fly began to circle above his head, buzzing noisily. The hunter waved at the fly in his sleep, tossing and turning, but the fly would not relent. The bear, whose one and only aim in life had become the constant care of his master-companion, couldn't succeed in waving off the fly either, and he became frustrated and impatient. The fly's incessant buzzing would not quiet down, adding to the bear's exasperation. In one great swoop the bear finally picked up the nearest rock that he could hold in his front paws and, as the fly alit on the hunter's forehead, slammed it onto the insect, crushing the hunter's skull along with the fly in one swift motion.

Such is the result of keeping company with the ignorant, albeit with the best of intentions.

Two Different Birds Flying Together

A physician regularly walked home through a field every evening after he had finished his house calls. His home lay underneath the path of migratory birds who spanned the sky while they flew to their respective destinations. He loved birds and often watched them closely when they flew overhead, trying always to observe their migrations.

Late one afternoon, the physician was tired after a long day but insisted on walking home rather than accepting a ride from a patient's son. As he strolled through the green countryside, he caught sight of two birds who were flying rather low, as if separated from their flock. They looked unusual, not the common birds who normally flew overhead at this time of year. He became curious and focused closely on this pair of birds.

They looked odd flying together for sure, because they were two different breeds! The physician had never seen anything like it and, after positively identifying the species, thought the matter through. He wondered to himself, how is it possible for the heavenly goshawk to fly with the earthbound owl? Why would a bird who belongs in Paradise accompany a bird who essentially belongs among the ruins of the earth?

Soon, the birds began to descend, preparing to land not far from where the physician had stopped to watch them. As they landed and began to hop toward what might have been a cluster of worms on the ground, the physician noticed that both birds were limping!

He had wondered how it was possible for two completely dissimilar birds to become companions, and now he had his answer: they were both lame in one leg, and that had become their binding factor! The poor goshawk, having suffered what appeared to have been a nearly fatal injury, had stooped to the level of the graveyard owl, abandoning his former majesty.

The Prophet Visits a Sick Man

An old acquaintance of the prophet Mohammad was taken ill. Unable to eat, he had lost a great deal of weight and become an invalid. When the prophet heard about his old friend's pitiful state, he decided to pay him a visit. As he walked into the sick man's room, he realized that the old man's days were numbered and that in fact he was nearing his end quite rapidly. Thus, he paid his friend much attention and tried to soothe his pain with kind words. The old man was so thrilled and grateful to see the prophet sitting beside him that he felt like he'd been gifted a new lease on life.

"My illness has brought me this unbelievable fortune!" he uttered feebly. "The prophet himself has come to pay me a visit! What an auspicious morning! How grateful I am for all my pains and aches, for they have brought the prophet to my side! God has bestowed me my wish in my old age. He has given me such a backache that I can't sleep at night from the pain, but this is no torture; it's in fact my treasure! My prayers have been answered before my death."

The prophet was puzzled when he heard the old man praying for pain.

"Old friend, from your words I can tell that you have been praying erroneously. You may have thought that you're asking God for sweet kindnesses, but in fact your wrong words have brought you much misfortune! It sounds like, instead of praying for a long, healthy life you've been begging for poisoned meals. Which prayer did you utter?"

"I can hardly remember, I'm in such agony," moaned the poor man. "But wait, being in your presence, my mind's beginning to clear a bit," he said weakly. "I felt guilty for many sins I'd committed and was frightened of God's punishment. I had no patience and felt unworthy to even begin to repent. Like a drowning man, I reached out to anything I could grab to keep afloat. I prayed that He would inflict all the tortures of hell upon me while I'm still alive so that once I pass into the next world I can finally find peace. Now I'm riddled with such pain and suffering that I can't even remember any prayers, let alone what my sins were! Your kind visit has meant a great deal to me, and

your words of comfort have brought me much joy. I thank you from the bottom of my heart."

The prophet looked at the man with great sorrow: "Be aware, and never again repeat such a prayer! Why would you want to cut off your roots with your own hands? You're no more than a minuscule, weak ant scurrying across the great scheme of life. Why would you invite the weight of a mountain to crush your back?" retorted the prophet.

"I repent, great prophet; I will never try to outsmart anyone again."

"When you pray to God, ask for an easier life to endure, not one that's more difficult than you can bear. Ask God for only goodness in this life, and in the next! Ask that your path cross through gardens lush with flowers guiding your way back to Allah, who should be your ultimate destination."

The prophet took leave after a few more minutes, knowing that the old man did not have much longer to live and wishing him a departure to a world that would be easier than the one he had conjured for himself on earth.

The Clown and the Prostitute

A member of the ruling family of the town of Termez had befriended a clown many years earlier. The two men had a compatible relationship, untarnished by the years. The clown made the older man laugh every time they saw each other, and the wealthy man in turn made sure that the clown was well provided for.

One day when they were alone, the older man, who had heard that the clown had recently got married to a woman of low standing and was baffled by this turn of events, asked him: "My old friend, there are many well-respected women in our community whom I know personally. Why didn't you tell me to ask for the hand of one of them for you? Why did you rush into such an important decision and marry a disreputable woman?"

"Sir, you must know that I have already married nine reputable women!" he said to his caring companion, trying not to grin too widely. "You may have also noticed that not a single one of them remained faithful to me, and I had to divorce every single one! My heart was shattered each time, and I couldn't tolerate another cheating wife. So I decided to marry an already disgraced woman, without even knowing her, and take a chance on life. I've already tried my luck using my mind and my reasoning power; this time I'm trying out madness instead!"

The Wise Madman

A young man had determined that it was time to get married, but he was not entirely sure about his decision. Because he did not wish to make a grave mistake, knowing that the choice of a bride was probably the most important decision of one's life, he decided to consult with someone wiser than himself. He searched the entire town and asked everyone he knew until finally someone told him: "In our town, there's only one wise person, and he's the old man who plays with children!"

It didn't take long to find the wise man; in fact, it would be hard to miss him. There, in the middle of the town's main square, he spent his days chasing a group of young children while riding a long bamboo stick, pretending that it was his wild and unruly horse. When the young man spotted him from a distance, he took note that he'd better approach the man carefully. "Hello, great horseman, would you please veer your horse toward me for a minute?" he implored desperately.

"Be swift and state your business," the man replied in a formal tone. "As you can see, my horse is wild and fierce and will kick you if you make a silly move," he warned.

"I wish to get married but am inexperienced and need advice. What can you tell me about women? Which woman would be the best choice for me?" he asked humbly, not sure if he was actually going to get a decent answer.

"There are three kinds of women in the world," replied the horseman knowledgeably. "Two are great treasures indeed, but the third kind is the greatest of treasures both in this world and the next."

The young man was grateful but confused. "Would you mind expounding on your theories?" he asked politely.

"I will start with the first type, who will be entirely yours all your life; while the second type of woman will be yours only partially; and the third type will not belong to you at all! Now, move away before my horse kicks your shin and lames you," declared the old man as he turned his bamboo horse toward the children and began to gallop away.

"Please wait," implored the young man, still confounded. "Now that you've shared your invaluable wisdom, please tell me, what do you mean exactly?"

The horseman pulled his bridle and turned to face the inquirer. "All right, let me tell you clearly once and for all. The woman whose heart will be yours but only halfway is the widow. Although childless, she'll always hold onto the fond memories of her late husband. There's another type of woman who will never share her heart with you, and she's the widow with children. Every time she looks at them, she'll be reminded of the love she shared with their father. Undoubtedly the best woman of all, whose heart will be yours forever, is the woman who has never shared it with anyone before you. Now get out of my way before my horse knocks you out."

"Dear old man, I have one last question to ask. May I?"

"Go on then," he replied, a little annoyed.

"Your wisdom is unrivalled; why do you pretend to madness?"

"The townsmen wished to select me as their supreme judge, but I refused time and time again," he confessed. "Nevertheless, they insisted that there was no other wise man in town whom they could trust. They wouldn't leave me alone; therefore, I had no choice but to pretend that I'd lost my mind. Inside, though, I'm still the same. My mind is my spiritual treasure, and I'll never share it with the common folk!"

Having imparted his precious secret, the wise madman rode toward the gang of boys, who were impatient to continue their unfinished battle.

The Night Watchmen and the Drunk

It was past midnight, and the night watchmen were patrolling the neighborhood when they came across a drunk leaning up against a wall. One of them walked up to the man, patted him on the shoulder, and screamed in his ear: "Hey! Are you drunk? Tell me, quick, what have you been drinking?"

"Whatever was in that bottle over there," the drunk said, pointing to an empty bottle that had rolled away to the side.

"What was in the bottle? You know that alcohol is illegal in this town," yelled the watchman again.

"I drank what was in the bottle, officer," replied the drunk, slurring his words.

"I don't see anything in the bottle; tell me, quickly, what did you drink?"

"What was in the bottle, I told you."

The watchman realized that he was chasing his own tail and that conversation with this man would be useless. He decided that if he wanted to arrest the drunkard, he must try another approach.

"Open your mouth and say *ah*," he ordered the drunk, by now half asleep, hoping to smell the alcohol on his breath.

"Hu!"[3] sighed the drunken man happily.

"I ordered you to say *ah* and you blurt out *Hu*?" snapped the angry guard.

"I'm ecstatic, why should I say *ah*? *Ah* is a sound for sad people like you who've allowed their backs to get bent in two. People like me are always happy, and that's where my *Hu* comes from!"

"Don't try to get out of this mess with your stupid rhetoric. I'm not buying any of your false spirituality. No more arguing; stand up!" he ordered with authority, knowing well that if he didn't act fast he would soon be outmaneuvered.

"That's all right, you can go now; I'm done here," said the drunk.

"I told you to get up! You're drunk, and I must take you in."

"Leave me alone. How do you expect to steal the clothing off a naked

---

3 *Hu* is one of the ninety-nine names for Allah.

man?" reasoned the drunk. "If I'd any strength, I'd walk to my own home and not waste my time arguing with you! If I could reason like the wise, I'd be sitting in my shop doing business, you fool!"

The drunk squatted, leaning his back against the wall, and closed his eyes, instantly falling asleep. Seeing the hopelessness of this arrest, the night watchmen, exasperated, walked off and left him alone.

A Thief at Hand

In the middle of the night, a man heard footsteps in his home and quickly got out of bed to investigate. Sure enough, in his sitting room there stood a thief, his hands filled with valuable objects. Taking fright, the burglar dropped everything he had gathered and jumped out the window onto the street, while the owner of the house gave chase. The owner, who was young and a fast runner, scurried after the thief for a few blocks in the darkness until the thief could run no more. The owner grabbed him by the scruff of his neck and was about to drag him to the police station when he heard someone calling out to him.

"Come quickly, come and see the signs left by the thief who's ravaged your home!" screamed the unknown voice.

"What a kind and concerned citizen," thought the owner. "What if there's a second thief in my home who might hurt my wife and children? *That* damage can never be undone! What good would it do me if I tie up this man but lose the true culprit? If I don't listen to this stranger, I might regret it for a long time to come."

The owner quickly let go of the thief he had caught and rushed back home. Outside the house walls, in the dark, there stood the thief's partner waiting for the owner to come back.

"Thank you," gasped the owner when he saw the second thief. "You've done me a great service! Tell me, why were you calling me?"

"Let me show you the footprints of the thief; the bastard has run away in that direction," he said, pointing to his right. "If you chase him right away you might still be able to catch him."

"You idiot! What on earth are you talking about? I already *had* caught him! *You* tricked me into letting him go. I had the truth in my grip and you are now suggesting that I look for *signs*?"

"I'm well aware of the truth," said the second thief, feigning innocence. "I'm only trying to show you the signs of the truth!"

"You're certainly either a burglar yourself or a total ignoramus! No, I'm certain that in fact you *are* a thief and know exactly what the other chap was up to. My enemy was in my hands and you made me set him free, and now you're blabbering about the *truth*?"

Sometimes, the truth is much too obvious; people erroneously search for its signs while the real thing is staring them right in the face.

Four Indians in Prayer

The sun was at its zenith, and four devout Indian Moslems entered a mosque to perform the noon prayer. As they stood shoulder to shoulder, each with a different hope in his heart, they began to pray. Halfway through their prayer, the sound of the muezzin rose in the air, casting doubt in their minds whether they had been too hasty in beginning to pray. One of the four men turned to the muezzin caller and asked him: "Dear public crier, are you sure you're not late today calling out the muezzin?"

One of the Indians was quick to address his friend: "My dear fellow, what have you done? You spoke in the midst of praying, and now your prayer is annulled!"

The third Indian turned to the second and exclaimed: "Hey, why do you blame him? You did exactly the same and have now broken your own prayer!"

"Thank God I didn't blurt out needlessly like these three!" declared the fourth Indian. "I'm too clever to commit such stupid mistakes! My prayer is still valid!" he boasted, unaware of his own equally damaging shortfall.

Such was the manner in which the prayers of all four men, who had tried to outdo each other in their judgments, were annulled that day.

Setting an Example

The Oghuz Turkmens were wild and fierce warriors who had invaded Persia and continued to ravage the lands in the northern parts of the country. Their army eventually arrived at a remote village with the full intention of massacring its inhabitants, pillaging their possessions, and then leveling the entire place.

As they rummaged through the tiny, dilapidated huts, they found two elderly men, one of whom was the head of the village and the other his neighbor. The Turkmens hurriedly bound one of the men, intending to slaughter him.

"Great warriors of our time, why would you want to kill a poor old man like me?" implored the destitute man. "Why spill my innocent blood? Don't you see that I'm so impoverished that I'm practically naked to the bone? What possible good could my death bring you?" he pleaded as the warriors began to bind his hands and feet.

"We'll slit your throat and set an example so that the other man tells us where he's buried his gold," replied a soldier.

"What gold? He's even poorer than *me!*"

"We have informers who have guaranteed that he's hiding his treasure."

"We are both in the same situation, so why don't you kill *him* instead of me, and I promise to show you where I'm hiding *my* gold!" reasoned the old man, cleverly trying to avoid certain death.

The Old Man and the Physician

A man had been suffering for a long time from a variety of ailments, as one does in old age. One day, he finally managed to drag himself to his local doctor to seek help. He did not have much confidence in doctors and their advice, but he was at his wit's end and could no longer tolerate the pain that had spread throughout his frail body.

"I'm suffering mostly from loss of memory, dear doctor," he began his complaints feebly.

"Loss of memory is a result of aging, my dear man," decreed the young physician.

"I'm losing my sight rapidly. What can I do?" he continued.

"Loss of sight is from aging," replied the doctor.

"My backache is debilitating," moaned the old man.

"Back pain is also the result of old age, my good man," said the doctor coldly.

"Nothing I eat seems to taste pleasant anymore," complained the old patient.

"Weakness of the stomach also comes with old age."

"When I breathe, I don't seem to get enough oxygen in my lungs," he carried on.

"Shortness of breath is also from aging," declared the young doctor as a matter of fact. "Old age brings with it a host of pains, my ancient friend."

The old man, who had kept his anger at bay until then, finally lost his temper and snapped: "You idiot! Is this all you've learned from years of studying medicine? Haven't you learned that for every aliment, God has created a cure? You're an imbecile who has learned nothing!"

The cool doctor was annoyed but firmly responded to the old man's insults: "You're sixty years old, and this anger and fury is also the result of aging! With the passage of time, the body's organs begin to deteriorate and leave one with little tolerance for controlling one's patience or fury. Therefore, I will pretend that I have heard nothing of your insults," retorted the doctor, brushing aside the old man's angry remarks.

Having lost the opportunity to tap into a little compassion in his heart, the young doctor never saw the old man in his surgery again.

Juhi at the Funeral

The young Juhi was accompanying his father to a colleague's funeral. The dead man's son led the procession, walking in front of the casket while shedding tears and crying out in delirious grief after his cherished father:

"My darling father, where are they taking you? Are they going to bury your adored body in a grave and cover it with heaps of earth? Are they taking you to a dark and narrow house, with no carpets to cover the floors, not even a straw mat? Will they lay you down in a house where no light ever shines, where no bread gets baked? Will they leave you behind in a place where no aroma of cooking ever rises in the air, a house with no proper door at its entrance, no staircase to its rooftop? Will they lay you down somewhere where there is no neighbor to knock on your door to ask about you? How could you, who were so widely revered and respected, ever tolerate such a dark and harsh home?"

When Juhi heard the young man utter these words as he mourned his father's demise, he turned to his own father and asked sheepishly: "Father, are they taking the corpse to our house?"

"Don't be an idiot! What a stupid question!"

"But father, all the details that the young man is describing point to our house. Listen to him carefully and you'll see what I mean. He says that the house has no light and that no food ever gets cooked there; its door is broken, and it has no garden or even a rooftop! That's what our house is like!" insisted the young Juhi, but his words went unheeded by his unmindful father.

A Sackful of Pebbles

In the Arabian deserts, merchants used to travel on camels, carrying goods from one town to another, usually in large caravans. One day, a merchant was traveling with one such caravan when he came across a learned man, who approached him.

"Greetings, my good man, where are you coming from and where are you headed?" the learned man asked.

The merchant responded to the stranger candidly, whereupon he was asked about the load he was carrying.

"I've got one sack filled with wheat and the other with pebbles," he said proudly.

"Why pebbles?"

"For balance, of course. Why else?"

"Why don't you fill the other sack with half of the wheat rather than burden your camel with pebbles? This way, the poor beast's load will be half as heavy."

"Well done, my good man," exclaimed the merchant with surprise. "What a brilliant idea! Now tell me, being as clever as you are, instead of riding on a horse or a camel, why are you walking this rough route, torturing yourself?

The merchant dismounted from his camel to offer the wise man a ride, as he felt sorry for him, but first he thought to ask him a few personal questions.

"So, tell me, being so wise, would you happen to be a governor or a minister?"

"Oh no, I'm neither a governor nor a minister. Just take a look at my clothes! I'm no one, just one of the common folk."

"But you must own a few camels and cows at least, being as clever as you are."

"No cows nor any camels."

"You must own a shop then. What do you sell?"

"I own no shop nor have any goods to sell."

"But you're an insightful and intelligent man; in fact, you're probably an alchemist who can turn base metals into gold. Your knowledge is invaluable. Be honest, tell me the truth, how much money have you got on you?"

"My dear fellow, I haven't got a bean in the world. I walk barefoot and suffer constantly from hunger, hoping to come across people who might take pity on me and offer me a slice of dry bread," confessed the wise man. "My intelligence and insight have only brought me trouble and suffering."

"Go away!" screamed the merchant suddenly. "Get out of my sight before your cursed intelligence rubs off on me, too. Your knowledge will only bear disaster for anyone you encounter, so get going before I kick you unconscious! I'll keep my sacks as they are, thank you very much. I'd much rather carry a sackful of pebbles than listen to your miserable, useless advice. If you could benefit from your own knowledge, you already would have done so. So, go on and get lost, you miserable creature."

The merchant quickly mounted his camel, whipped and kicked her mightily, and urged her to speed away as quickly as possible from the supposedly wise man.

God Will Not Punish Me

One day as Jethro, Moses's father-in-law, was busy with his daily chores, a friend he had not seen for a long time stopped by to have a cup of tea. As they spoke about this and that, the man began to boast about his luck.

"I've committed countless sins in my life, but God never punishes me, because He's benevolent!" he said proudly.

Jethro was baffled and wondered why his friend had told him what he had. Not long after, he had a revelation in which God spoke to him:

"Tell this unknowing man to stop claiming that I have not punished him for his sins. It's indeed the opposite! I have grabbed him and held him in my hands many times, but he was completely incognizant of it. Tell him that he's become so tainted inside and out, like a blackened pot, that darkness no longer has any effect on him. Patches of dirt are immediately apparent on a clean surface; it's the same with sin and the marks it leaves on the soul. Darkness first strikes at the inside and then reveals itself slowly on the outside.

"When someone's whole being has been tainted through and through, he's unable to understand or even see that he's only adding to his impurity every day. One could of course repent and ask for forgiveness, and relief may be forthcoming, but when one's heart has been so irreparably tarnished, then one has lost all predisposition for repentance."

After hearing God's words, Jethro repeated them to the man the next time they met, hoping to convince him of his errant ways, but he was surprised when the man replied good-naturedly: "So tell me, Jethro, if God has caught me in his snare, then where are His signs?"

Jethro was exasperated and later confided in God that the poor soul did not believe his words. God spoke kindly to Jethro, relieving him of his duty as a messenger in this case.

"I'm the Master Concealer," decreed God. "But I will not share my wisdom with this unconscious creature. I'll tell you one thing, though, Jethro: it's true that this man is adamant about performing his prayers and fasting, and

he even willingly pays his religious taxes. However, his deeds are not honest and don't come from his heart! His faith has no essence. What appears on the outside is pleasing, but in reality he's a fraud. To have enthusiasm in one's heart for spirit is the essential seed for growth, which this man lacks entirely."

Jethro did not question what had been revealed to him, and the next time he met his old friend, he smiled knowingly and kept his silence.

Camel and Mouse

A merchant had been traveling all day long, and it was late afternoon when he arrived at the caravansary, completely exhausted. He dismounted his camel and vigilantly unloaded the burden it was carrying but was careless when he tied the bridle to a post before walking inside the adjacent building to rest for the night.

Soon afterward, the bridle loosened, and the camel began to walk away. A little desert mouse spotted the bridle twisting like a snake on the ground and quickly took it in her mouth and ran in front of the large beast. The camel, who was bored, thought that the little mouse was entertaining and decided not to whip his bridle out of her grip, allowing her to lead him on. The mouse was chuffed, believing that she was in charge of guiding the mighty camel, and began to feel proud of her unrivaled abilities.

"What a great hero I am!" she thought contentedly. "Just look at me pulling such a huge animal behind me!"

The camel noticed that pride was rising in the mouse's heart but feigned ignorance and allowed her to arrogantly continue pulling his bridle.

"I'll let her enjoy her moment of splendor; who knows what the future holds," he said to himself philosophically.

The pair continued their journey for some time until they arrived at a wide stream, which seemed like an endless river to the mouse. She climbed upon a mound of dirt to see if she could spot the opposite bank, but it was too far away to be visible. The camel was well aware of why the mouse was stalling but pretended not to have noticed.

"Hey, little mouse, why have you stopped?" he asked her smugly. "Don't be a halfway friend, let's get going," he urged her on.

"My friend, the water is too deep and too fast! I'm afraid of drowning," she exclaimed helplessly.

"Let me check it out," said the camel gallantly as he stepped into the water. "You're such a twat; this water isn't deep at all! Look, it only comes up to my knees!"

"This water may seem as insignificant as a small gathering of ants to you, but to me it's as impassable as a row of ferocious dragons! Your knee and mine are quite different in height, can't you see?" she pleaded.

"Perhaps you shouldn't have been so audacious and had found another mouse your own size to lead instead of hoping to master the mighty camel!" he exclaimed emphatically.

"I repent, I repent," repeated the mouse sincerely. "Help me cross this water, and I'll never let myself be ruled by my pride again."

The camel felt pity for the little mouse.

"Hurry up and climb onto my hump," he exclaimed sympathetically. "Crossing this stream is simple for me; in fact, I could carry hundreds like you in one crossing!"

And so the camel and the mouse continued their symbiotic companionship for the rest of their days together.

Shaykh on the Boat

There was once a shaykh who looked nothing like a high Sufi; his clothes were in tatters and he appeared gaunt and undernourished. One year, he was obliged to go to a city that lay beyond the sea, and therefore he had no choice but to travel by boat. As he was generally destitute, he boarded a luxury boat but took refuge among the cargo. As the boat pulled away from the harbor, the gentle rocking soon lulled the shaykh into a deep slumber.

Not long after the boat began to sail, a man on board began to holler and curse, for his pouch of gold coins had disappeared. The captain ordered every passenger to be searched and searched again. Soon it was the turn of the shaykh, who was still sound asleep resting among the passengers' luggage. The sailors reluctantly woke up the poor man and informed him of the situation, ordering him to remove all his clothes so they could make sure he was not the culprit.

The shaykh was embarrassed and deeply hurt.

"My Lord," he turned to the heavens and begged his Master. "These mischievous infidels are accusing Your humble servant of robbery. I beg of You to order them to release me and take back their baseless allegations."

The shaykh's heart had been broken by the callousness of his fellow passengers and nothing could appease him, until he saw a miracle appear in the broad sea that surrounded them. Millions of glittering fish poked their heads out of the water, flapping their tails vigorously to hold themselves upright, each holding a precious pearl in her mouth worth the entire treasury of a wealthy kingdom! The shaykh leaned over the side of the boat and collected a few pearls from some nearby fish, nonchalantly tossing the pearls onto the deck.

Then, like a crowned king seated on his throne, he levitated in air above the moving boat. He turned his face toward the passengers and announced: "You can have your boat with all its luxury, but I prefer the company of my God instead. I'll leave you now so that you don't have to travel alongside a thief. We shall soon see who benefits the most from this separation. I choose

to pull away from you to join with God, who will never accuse me of any wrongdoing nor leave me in the hands of unworthy liars and accusers."

The passengers were awestruck and implored the shaykh to tell them how he had managed to rise to such a glorious stature.

"I've never doubted the words of darvishes and shaykhs to begin with!" he stated reproachfully. "I've never accused the poor of wrongdoing, nor have I ever bothered God with the trifling affairs of this world, like you have!"

Before the passengers could ask him anything further, the shaykh vanished into thin air, as if he had never been there at all.

Reprimanding a Darvish

One day, a group of Sufis went to their shaykh to complain about one of their fellow darvishes. "Master, we need your help," they pleaded. "Please save us from this man's company, for he'll soon put an end to us all."

"What's your complaint, dear fellows?" asked the shaykh sympathetically.

"This chap is supposed to be a proper Sufi, but he suffers from three major character flaws," one of the darvishes protested. "When he speaks, it's like a siren going off, loud and unremitting. When he eats, he polishes off the portions of twenty men! And when he sleeps, oh my God when he sleeps, it's as if he'll never wake up again!"

The shaykh listened to his students patiently and in due time called the unpopular man to his presence. He kindly advised him to change his ways and always adopt the middle path, never exaggerate in his behavior. The man listened to his spiritual master quietly, trying to grasp the essence of what he was being told. The master shaykh realized that this was a great opportunity to impart essential Sufi teachings, interweaving them with his advice.

"When people exaggerate, they eventually become ill," said the shaykh with gravity. "One must always cooperate with one's fellow Sufis; otherwise, separation and alienation will result. With the masses, Moses always spoke just enough, but with close friends he elaborated his thoughts much more freely. Once when he rambled on a bit too long with the prophet Khidr, he was scolded and sent away, rebuked for having spoken far too much! If he wanted to stay in Khidr's company, he was told that he would have to remain mute and blind. Now, my good man, if you, too, continue with your excessive behavior, you'll ultimately alienate all your friends!"

The shaykh felt that his words were slowly penetrating the young Sufi's consciousness and decided to seize the moment and continue with his spiritual advice.

"You're still a young Sufi; choose your companions carefully. Find the ones who thirst for your words. Try to live like a naked man, without any embellishment or decoration. Seek the company of those who are free of these

vanities, too. And if you can't completely strip naked, then at least lighten your load, remove your extra layers and adopt a balanced state of being."

The young Sufi exclaimed his gratitude and paid his shaykh great courtesy, and then he asked permission to speak. "The middle path, my great shaykh, is relative," he said. "The water in a shallow stream may seem hardly an obstacle to the camel, but to the mouse it's a vast and swollen sea. When someone has an appetite for four loaves of bread, he must consume at least two or three loaves. For someone who can only appease his hunger with ten loaves, he can perhaps manage with a minimum of six. I personally can easily eat fifty loaves of bread, so six loaves seem like nothing to me.

"One man may tire after saying ten prayers, but I've the stamina to recite, without a break, at least five hundred prayers. One person might be brave and selfless and give up his life willingly for a worthy cause, while another man will give up his life before submitting to part with a single loaf of bread!"

The young man fell silent and lowered his head respectfully before his shaykh. The shaykh, too, remained silent.

"Ah, and when it comes to sleep," remembered the Sufi, "I may sleep for hours on end, but my heart is perpetually awake. One should be wary of those whose bodies are restless but whose hearts are chronically numb. My heart gazes into both worlds, and I can clearly see how many people get stuck in the mud while I glide over it with ease. I may be cohabiting with them on the earth, but I walk in the heavens.

"I've surpassed plain thoughts and have gone far beyond. As I take to the air, I leave mundane ruminations behind. It is I who choose to descend, so that these lame devotees of yours may benefit from my presence."

He kissed the edge of his shaykh's robe, stepped away without showing his back to his master, and quietly walked out of the room.

The Tree of Eternal Life

A learned man who had traveled the world over was heard telling a story about a tree in India whose fruit bestowed eternal life. The story was brought to the attention of the king, who, like most people, desired to live forever, and he instantly became obsessed with finding the tree. He ordered one of his most trusted ministers to travel to India in search of the special fruit and gave him ample funds to support his travels.

Upon arrival in India, the minister began his thorough search from the southernmost point of the subcontinent to the remotest mountains in the north. He traveled from town to town and from village to village, asking every person he came across about the tree and its fruit. Most people laughed in his face, taking him for an imbecile, while others just ignored him as they would a madman. The minister spent many lonely days and nights in foreign places, only rarely coming across a friendly face. If anyone did speak to him earnestly, it was to convince him to give up his useless search, to tell him that he was wasting his precious life. Some people would tease him and give him false directions to an imaginary tree in some difficult location, making him go off his trail and wasting more of his time. Mostly, though, people just laughed at him and took him for a fool.

The devoted minister, however, did not give up, pressing on with his mission tirelessly. To ensure that he did not quit, the king regularly sent him sufficient funds to support him. Years passed, and the minister turned gray and old, and he finally had to admit that he had failed. With tearful eyes, he began his journey back home after years of absence and hardship.

On his way back, he decided to pay a visit to a learned shaykh whom he had heard about, hoping to receive a blessing from him. However, the minute his eyes met the shaykh's, he burst into tears, sobbing uncontrollably for quite some time. Once he managed to take control of his senses, he confessed to the holy man: "Great shaykh, I've lost my way! I haven't achieved what I set out to achieve all those years ago, and now I'm returning to my master shamefaced and empty-handed. I beg of you to take pity on me and show me the right path."

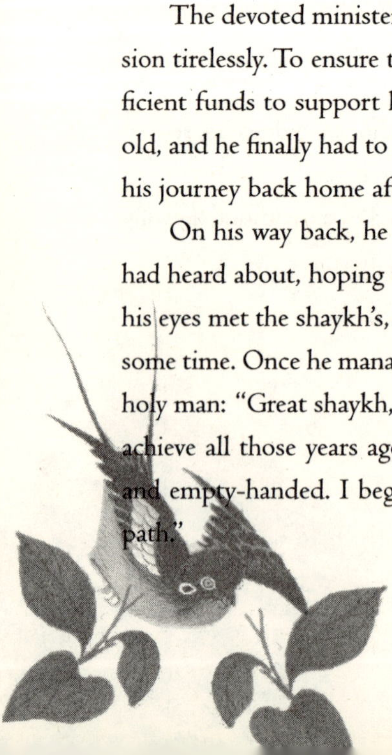

"What are you searching for, my good man?" asked the shaykh with compassion.

"Years ago, my king sent me in search of a tree that produces a fruit that gives eternal life. I've wasted my youth searching for it, but I never found it. All I found was sarcasm and pity!" whimpered the minister.

"My wise man, this tree you speak of is the Tree of Knowledge, which grows within the human heart!" imparted the shaykh benignly. "You've been searching for what's readily apparent, and in the process, you've given up on the real meaning of life. This phenomenon is called by different names; one calls it the sea, another calls it a cloud, while another calls it a tree or even the sun, and many more names besides. Knowledge has thousands of uses, one of which is eternal life! God is one and without a rival, but He gives forth infinite signs. Think about it: a man may be your father, but he's also someone's son; what may seem like anger in the eyes of an enemy is kindness to a friend.

"You've been saddled with only one of His signs, namely the tree that you've been seeking. If you don't want to remain defeated, it's time for you to ignore what you see on the surface and begin to concentrate on the essence. What creates differences between men is precisely this superficiality, but once they understand what lies beneath the surface, duality vanishes."

The minister felt an immense burden lifted from his shoulders; he no longer felt dejected or defeated. His heart had opened, and he knew that his passage back home would be one of joy rather than grief.

Grapes for Four

Four men had been traveling in the same caravan all day long but had not spoken a word to one another. When their convoy stopped for the evening, the four men made a fire together and warmed themselves as they gathered around it.

The men were from four different countries, and none spoke the others' languages. They were Persian, Arab, and Turkish, and the fourth man, a Greek speaker, was from the Sultanate of Rûm. They were laborers in tattered clothes who looked destitute. As they sat huddled together, shaking like leaves in the chill air, one of their fellow travelers, who was better off, took pity and offered them a small sum of money so they could buy something to eat.

The Persian was quick to suggest: "Let's spend our money on grapes."

"What a creep! I don't want what he wants, I want grapes," said the Arab defiantly.

"No, my dear fellows," complained the Turk, "I don't like what you've suggested; I prefer grapes."

"Come on guys, don't argue. It's best if we all agree to buy grapes," concluded the man from Rûm in Greek.

Not understanding each other, the men began fighting, throwing punches and cursing in their own respective tongues. As the men fought among each other, a wise and holy man saw them from afar and quickly approached them. Succeeding in separating them, he managed to find out what their problem was, as he was fluent in all four languages. Thanks to the wisdom of the sage, the grapes were soon acquired, relieving the four unwitting men from the burden of their rage.

The Duckling

A storm had dislodged a cluster of duck eggs from the safety of the tree-lined shore, where their mother had created a safe haven for them in the shade. As they floated purposelessly over the foaming waves, one of the eggs got caught in a whirlpool and was separated from the others. Under the pressure of the swirling water, the shell broke, and a little duckling poked his head out, trying to breath in the new air. The relentless waves, however, tossed the cracked egg onto the unfriendly shore, separating him forever from the other eggs.

The tiny duckling struggled to emerge from the cracked shell and finally managed to waddle away from the devouring sea onto dry sand. Unable to fend for himself, the little duckling felt abandoned and frightened. As luck would have it, a hen whose eggs had just hatched was nearby and saw the helpless creature rolling around feebly on the endless expanse of shore. She approached him and with great kindness sheltered him under her wing, taking him to her own chicks.

The newborns grew up together and were able to nourish themselves without the aid of their mother hen fairly quickly. The duckling, though, always found himself drawn to the water but was too frightened to go in, as he saw that none of his siblings had any desire to even try. He was torn inside, unable to comprehend why he felt the way he did. Some days he only wanted to be on dry land, but other days all he wanted was to get wet.

Although he couldn't fully understand his own nature, at the same time he couldn't deny it either; much like we humans, who belong to the spirit world and always yearn to go back but are caught in the snare of the material world, unable to fully detach ourselves.

MASNAVI III

Elephant Eaters

A group of men had been on the road in India for days without food or water. Unfamiliar with the terrain they were covering and unable to feed themselves, they became desperately undernourished. Nevertheless, they continued on their journey, famished and distraught but determined to reach their final destination.

In a twist of luck, a learned man who had traveled in that area many times before and was familiar with the wildlife of the region happened to cross their path. Looking at the condition of their clothing and their pale faces, he quickly concluded that they were hungry strangers and felt compelled to warn them about the elephants that roamed the land.

"Greetings my good men, I can see that you're tired and hungry, for there's not much prey in these parts," he commiserated. "But beware that elephants roam freely in this area, and their young, who are plump, sometimes get separated from their mothers and are then easily caught. You must never, ever try to hunt an elephant calf, though, for his mother will find you no matter how many miles you may think you've traveled from where you caught the calf. She will sniff out her child's scent on you, and she'll trample you to death the moment she catches up. Mark my words and stick to eating herbs and fruits, if you find them!"

The exhausted men listened to the wise man's words, thanked him for his advice, and continued on their journey. Desperately hungry, they looked under every shrub and up every tree that might bear fruit, but they found nothing edible. Suddenly, one of the men spotted an elephant calf who had been separated from his clan. Without hesitation, the men, except for one who heeded the wise man's advice, attacked the young beast and, facing minimal resistance, killed him on the spot.

Too famished to listen to the learned man's warnings, the men quickly started a fire and cooked the plump animal, feasting on his flesh. Having satisfied their hunger at last, they washed their hands and faces in a stream nearby and promptly fell asleep on the banks. The conscientious man who had not

participated in the slaughter or touched a morsel of the flesh decided to stay awake and guard their camp, instinctively feeling that the wise man had not warned them without good reason.

Meanwhile, the mother elephant had been searching everywhere for her young one, growing more furious and exasperated by the minute. Sniffing everything with her long, sturdy trunk, she eventually detected her offspring's scent in the near distance and quickened her step. In a wink of an eye, she was upon the felons' camp. She approached the one man who was awake and sniffed him from head to toe, especially around his mouth, to see if she could detect the scent of her baby. The man was immobile, tongue-tied with fright. She circled him three times to make sure she had not made a mistake and then passed him by without harming him, quickly going to the other men sleeping a little farther away.

She sniffed the first man's mouth and immediately smelled her baby, then crushed him under her forelegs, the size of stone pillars, and threw him up in the air with her mighty trunk, breaking virtually every bone in his body. Then she approached the others who had feasted on her child, and, one by one, subjected them to the same excruciating treatment without showing the least sign of remorse.

When the last guilty man had been slaughtered, the mother elephant returned to the man who had refrained from eating her offspring. She graciously knelt down before him and in one quick swoop lifted him with her trunk onto her back and gallantly carried him to his final destination.

The Painted Jackal

A scrawny jackal was ambling on his own when he slipped and fell into a puddle of paint. He splashed and rolled around happily for a while until he got tired and decided to walk back to his pack. As he stepped out of the puddle, he noticed that he was now covered in a variety of colors: his left side was red, his right side was yellow, his paws were white, his tail was green, and his chest was blue. Turning his head around from side to side toward his own frame, he began to admire himself, surmising that he had become more beautiful than even the heavenly looking peacock.

Proudly and coquettishly, he wandered in among his fellow jackals, pretending not to notice how they stared at him skeptically. Self-importantly, the jackal ignored his old friends, quickly adopting a haughty attitude toward them. The jackals who had known him since they were puppies were hardly impressed with his new behavior. "What on earth are these colors you've painted yourself with?" they asked him. "You're so engrossed with your new look that it seems you've forgotten your lifelong friends. Remember, you're nothing more than a plain jackal, just like the rest of us. What's gone into your head? Why all this unfounded pride all of a sudden?"

The painted jackal ignored their comments and continued to strut his attitude. One of the jackals who knew him better than the others approached him nonchalantly: "What's going on? What've you got up your sleeve? Are you playing at tricking us or do you simply want to stir our jealousy so you can manipulate us later?" He concluded: "You can see that none of us are impressed with you. In fact, no one is paying you any attention! No doubt you'll soon show your true colors!"

The jackal didn't climb down from his high horse, instead pompously urging: "Have a good look at my dazzling colors! Have you ever, in your entire life, come across such an outstanding idol? I've become like a garden of enchanting flowers, blossoming in hundreds of colors. Observe my grace and beauty and kneel before my majesty. The world is a more glorious place

because I exist, for I'm a sign of God's graciousness. I've become a tablet brimming with His beauty."

He then turned to face the other jackals and spat out: "You lowly beasts, don't you ever dare call me a jackal again. When was a jackal ever as magnificent as I?"

The jackals circled around him and asked: "If not a jackal, then what should we call you?"

"I'm the exquisite male peacock, as lustrous as Jupiter!"

"If you're a peacock, then let's hear your unrivaled, piercing song," they demanded shrewdly.

"No, no, no! Singing I cannot do!"

The jackals all burst into loud laughter and walked away from the delusional painted jackal, shaking their heads in amusement at his inept mind.

Elephant in the Dark

In a faraway region, there was a remote town built purely by the sweat of its inhabitants' brows. The people of this town had never seen an elephant before, and when Hindus arrived with their majestic animal, it was indeed a novel event. The elephant was a prized possession, and the Hindu owners insisted that he be kept indoors to spare him from the cold desert night. Thus, the glorious animal was kept in the largest structure the inhabitants could provide.

The townspeople were thrilled when they discovered that the owners of the noble beast had brought him to put on a show in every town they passed through. They insisted on seeing the elephant that same evening despite the owners' emphatic insistence that the animal could not be viewed properly in the dark. However, the townspeople did not mind the darkness, and they were willing to pay extra. They were adamant that they couldn't wait until the following morning and had to see the animal that very first night. At last the owners relented and allowed the people to enter the stable but insisted that they had to go inside one by one, as the elephant was taking up most of the space inside the structure.

The first viewer walked in cautiously and felt the elephant's trunk. "This animal resembles a pipe!" he declared when he stepped outside.

The second person stepped in and began to caress the elephant's ear. "No, this beast is like a big fan!" he reported.

The third curious person walked in and pressed his palms against the elephant's strong and sturdy legs, exclaiming as he stepped out: "What fan? This elephant is as robust as a pillar!"

The fourth man, who was very tall, entered the enclosure and began to run his hands over the elephant's back. "This creature is as flat as a bed!" he said with disappointment.

As more and more people walked inside the dark room, each one came out with a different understanding of the phenomenon they had encountered. None of them were able to truly find out what the elephant actually looked like, for they were in the dark and had to rely on the acute limitations of their imperfect senses.

The Grey Beard

The barber had just opened his shop and was sweeping the floor when a man rushed in and demanded to be served.

"Good morning, my good sir," said the barber politely. "How can I be of service?"

"Good morning," hurried the man. "Please, quickly, can you separate and cut out the white hairs in my beard? I've just taken a young bride, and she doesn't like my gray look."

The barber took a quick look at the customer, who had already sat down in the barber's chair, ready for his shave. He noticed that the man's beard was not just "salt and peppery" but in fact nearly all white. He took out his razor and shaved the man's entire beard off in one quick motion, then laid it before him, commenting disdainfully: "Here's your beard; you can separate the gray yourself! I've got work to do."

The barber then turned his back on the customer and continued with his sweeping.

The Sound of the Slap

A man was sitting quietly on a bench, minding his own business, when a younger man plopped himself down heavily beside him. Before the first man could turn to see who had just sat down, the other man slapped him loudly on the back of the neck. The first man was outraged and instinctively turned to defend himself by tackling his assailant, when the young man said philosophically: "Please, please, wait a second before you slap me back! Can you just tell me something: when I slapped you, did you hear how loud it was? So, do you suppose that the sound came from my *hand*, which delivered the slap, or was it your neck that made that loud sound?"

The first man grew even more furious and snapped back: "You idiot, who cares?" He continued, hot with impatience: "I'm twisting and burning with pain, and you're wondering where the sound came from? Have you got nothing better to do than make a nuisance of yourself and waste people's time?"

Wisely deciding not to waste his own time with such a fool, he stood up from the bench, threw one last disdainful look at the useless philosophizing stranger, and walked away, rubbing his neck tenderly.

The Love Letter

A young couple in love had been separated from each other for over a year. The young man had suffered greatly and written many long, heart-wrenching letters to his beloved, complaining about his sorry state of mind and heart. One early morning, he walked into a lush garden near the girl's home and, as luck would have it, the girl was there, too. He didn't miss a beat and quickly approached her, noting that her old nanny, who usually accompanied her, was absent.

Thrilled that after so long a time he was able to sit by her side and hold her soft gaze, he took out copies of his love letters, which he carried with him at all times, and began to read them out loud. He recounted over and over again how much he had suffered day and night, how his lips had not touched a morsel of food, how his eyes had been wet with tears every single day. The girl took a few minutes to gather her thoughts and realized what her beloved was doing.

"When you've already written all these words to me, why are you repeating yourself and wasting our precious little time together?" she said with obvious pain in her tone. "I'm sitting here next to you, and you're reading love letters to me? This isn't the behavior of someone in love!"

The boy, taken aback, responded in disbelief: "I don't seem to recognize the same girl I knew last year! I drank from her fresh spring a year ago and bathed my eyes and heart in her crystal-clear water. I can still see the spring, but there's no water! Has a thief perhaps redirected the stream?"

"I'm not the one you love, my dear!" exclaimed the girl downheartedly. "I belong to one side of the world and you to the other. You're only in love with the state of being in love, not with me! You're attached to me hoping to experience that state once again. This isn't true love. The true lover is as one with his beloved; his beginning and end are contained in her beginning and end. They're one and the same. If you truly seek pure love, keep on searching, for that's the only water that will quench your thirst for a lifetime. *That* is the original fountain of purity that your soul has been reaching for, not *me*!"

She stood up, took one last look at the young man's stunned face, and quietly walked away.

Students and Teacher

The students were exasperated by their dreadfully strict teacher, who never allowed them a moment's respite. Every day, they conjured up naughty plans to distract him but somehow never managed to fool him. One day, the cleverest of the boys, who was also the most streetwise, came up with a brilliant plan. As his classmates gathered around him after school, he explained to them:

"Tomorrow morning when we come to school, I'll approach the master first and ask him how he feels and why he's looking so pale. I'll wish him well and say that he should take better care of himself. Then, you all should follow my lead and one after the other repeat the same questions so that we can instill doubt in his heart. After the fifth or sixth person, surly he must begin to wonder whether we've got a point or not. When thirty of us have told him the same thing, he'll have no choice but to believe us and let us off school at least for a couple of days."

The boys were all excited and commended the clever boy for his astute idea. The boy made them all promise not to tell their parents and stick to their scheme. The next morning, the students were all on time and awaited the arrival of the clever boy, for they could not begin their plot without him. As soon as he arrived, they nodded to each other and one by one entered the classroom.

"Good morning to you, sir. Are you all right sir? Why do you seem so pale this fine morning?" said the clever boy to the teacher cunningly.

"I'm perfectly fine. What are you blabbering about? Go sit down in your seat," the teacher ordered the boy in his usual abrasive manner.

The first seed of doubt had been planted. The students then walked into the classroom one after the other and each addressed the teacher in turn, commenting with concern on the latter's health. Despite his repeated denials, the teacher slowly began to believe the boys, as he had heard the same remark about his pale countenance thirty times. He began to shiver and actually feel feverish. Soon, he was hastily packing his papers and books and hurrying home, with thirty boys in tow.

All the way home, he was thinking about how his wife had recently been neglecting him, and how despite all his kindness and generosity she'd been wishing him ill. Entertaining these negative thoughts about his innocent wife, the teacher hastened through the narrow backstreets to his humble home, while the boys followed him closely every step of the way.

He slammed the front door noisily, intending thus to announce his untimely arrival to his wife as he entered their house. When she saw that he had returned from school so early, she quickly approached him and inquired about his health.

"Are you blind? Don't you see how sick I am? You're such a hypocrite! You can very well see how awful I'm feeling, yet you pretend that nothing's the matter with me!" he retorted.

"My darling, what are you saying? You must be suffering from delusions. Nothing is the matter with you!" his wife said, trying to appease his anger.

"You're despicable; you're a horrid woman! Can't you see my sorry state? Is it my fault that you're blind and deaf to my needs?" he continued, cruelly slandering his wife.

"I'm going to bring you the mirror so you can see for yourself that nothing's the matter with you."

"To hell with your mirror! You've always hated me and wished me the worst. Go and prepare my bed, I need to rest!"

The woman was stunned, unable to move or decide what she should do, when her husband screamed at her: "Get going, you good-for-nothing! Do you want me to pass out right here?"

The woman decided to remain quiet and do as he asked; otherwise, he might indeed think that she had foul intentions, and he could truly turn nasty. Thus, she prepared his bedding on the floor and left him with his students, who had accompanied him into the house. The boys gathered around his bed and began to review their lesson loudly, having been instructed by their ringleader to make as much noise as possible to exacerbate their teacher's fantasy headache.

"Quiet!" snapped the teacher. "Quiet, I said! Go home. Leave me in peace."

The students were free at last; wishing their teacher all the health in the world, they practically flew out of his house. They didn't go home, though, and instead remained in the streets, playing various games that they'd long fantasized about. Their mothers, however, soon found out that their sons had skipped school, and when they found them on the streets they reprimanded them, refusing to accept that they'd been excused by their teacher. They threatened to visit the teacher's home the next day and find out the truth. And so they did. They found the poor man lying miserably under several duvets, sweating like a pig and moaning in pain.

"Dear sir, forgive us, for we didn't believe our sons," confessed the women. "Now we can see for ourselves how ill you really are! May God grant you a long, healthy life."

"I'm actually grateful to your perceptive sons for having detected my malady," said the teacher gratefully. "I was so intent on teaching them that I had totally ignored my own health. If it hadn't been for them, I'd have soon been dead for certain!"

And such was the fate of the ignorant teacher, who'd been fooled by baseless repetition and indoctrination conducted by mere children.

The Wise Goldsmith

The goldsmith opened the shutters of his shop as usual, unlocked the door, and immediately began to sweep the floor. He hated having to work in a dusty environment, and it had become his habit for years to do one round of sweeping every morning, even though his assistant was responsible for the upkeep of the shop. That morning, shortly after he finished cleaning up, an old man walked in, a small pouch in his hand.

"Good morning, my good man. Can you please lend me your scale so I can weigh my gold scraps?" he asked politely.

"Go on your way, old man. I've no sieve, no broom, and no time to sift through your stuff!"

"What? Are you mocking me? I asked you for a simple scale," retorted the old man.

"I told you, I've no broom nor a sieve in the shop."

"I asked you for a scale. I didn't ask for a broom or a sieve! What are you rambling on about?"

The goldsmith, who was an old hand at his business, looked the old man in the eyes and tried his best to be kind:

"I heard you the first time, my dear fellow! I'm not deaf, and don't even think that I might be dumb. You, however, are old and your hands shake. Your gold is in small pieces, almost as fine as powder! With one errant shake of your hand, the whole batch will be on the floor. Then you'll ask me for a broom to sweep up the gold, which will now be mixed in with the dust from the floor. Next, you'll be asking me for a sieve to clear out the dust. From that very first moment you stepped into my shop, I could see the end result of our encounter! Please don't give me any trouble and go on your way!" concluded the wise goldsmith, who by now was holding the door open for the old man to take his leave.

The Basket Weaver

There was once a Sufi shaykh who had no arms, yet he managed to weave baskets for a living. He never shared his secret with anyone and generally remained aloof from people. He lived on his own, up in the mountains that loomed over the town. One day, as he was busily weaving a new basket—with both arms and hands intact—a man stumbled into his hut.

"Have you lost your mind?" the Sufi rebuked the intruder. "Why did you rush into my home like a madman? Who gave you permission to enter?"

"Forgive me, master, I was overawed and lost control!" replied the young seeker, obviously distressed that he had unsettled the old man.

The old basket weaver smiled gently and told him: "Now that you've seen my secret, promise me that until I die you'll never divulge it to anyone, be it friend or foe."

As he uttered these words, he noticed a group of people hunched outside the window of his hut. They had heard him ask the young novice to keep his secret, and they had seen him weaving his basket using his own arms and hands. He knew that his secret was out but could not understand the reason for this intrusion into his quiet and devoted life. Trusting in God and His wisdom, the old man continued with his weaving, ignoring the intruders whenever they happened to walk by. His prayers for an explanation were soon answered through a revelation:

"As you quietly carried on with your work, a group of untrusting townsfolk circulated rumors that you are a liar and impostor. I did not wish them to be considered infidels and be accused of questioning God's miracles. Therefore, I made them privy to your secret. I wished them to see with their own eyes the miracle that you can weave with both hands, so that they always trust and believe in God and be spared from eternal ignorance."

Relieved that he was safe in his solitude, the old master continued weaving his baskets until the day he died.

Not Mourning the Dead

Years ago, there was a Sufi shaykh, righteous and holy, who was revered by all. As it happened, an unknown illness took the lives of two of his children. His household, the entire neighborhood, indeed people from far and away mourned this calamity for weeks on end. The only person who never shed a tear was the shaykh himself. Much time passed, but still there were no tears, no signs of mourning. People were perplexed, unable to decipher what had happened to their favorite holy man. At last a devotee gently approached him: "Forgive my intrusion, great shaykh, but we're all in a state of disbelief," she said sheepishly.

"How can I help you, my dear?" inquired the shaykh, looking up from his reading.

"How can you remain so aloof and unfeeling about the loss of your darling children, while grief over their tragedy has bent our backs in double? You're our leader and master whom we trust intrinsically, and we ultimately hope to find solace in you during our own illness and demise. Why this silence? Don't you feel any pain? Perhaps you've no compassion left in your heart! How can we continue to hope for your guidance in our hour of need?"

On and on she pestered the shaykh, who remained silent, allowing her to speak her mind and relieve herself of the disappointment she felt. When she finally finished, the shaykh gently explained: "My dear girl, don't imagine for a moment that I'm void of compassion and love. I feel empathy even for sinners; I've compassion even for rocks and stones, which can injure people! Even dogs who bite us get my sympathy, and I pray that God may relieve them of this particular foul habit!"

"When you feel such mercy for strangers and offer them guidance like the good shepherd you are, how come you don't mourn the loss of your own children? Tears are a sign of kindness and love, yet your eyes are never moist like ours."

The shaykh turned his face to the woman and said: "My good woman, let me tell you, winter is not like the summer! Although my children are gone, they're not absent before my heart's eyes; in fact, they're very much alive. When I see them living joyfully like this, how can I scratch my eyes out like you do? They may not be present at this time, but I can see them playing all around me. They cry when they feel the separation between us, but I'm always with them. Some people may see them in their dreams, but I see them while I'm awake. I've let go of the senses and hide myself from the people of this world, and that's how I can observe everyone in silence. Having such a treasure, why should I be shedding tears needlessly?"

Valuable Advice

During the prophet's lifetime, people would travel from faraway lands to pay him their respects in person, often enduring much hardship on their journey. Generally, people came with their problems, and they always left with valuable advice that turned their lives around for the better.

One day, the prophet was busy with his usual daily tasks when one of his old followers, who had not seen him for a while, approached him. At first, the follower was reluctant to discuss his predicament with the great man, as he was embarrassed to confess to his shortcomings. After beating around the bush for a while, he finally presented his dilemma.

"I desperately need to hear your insight, my honorable friend," he said, swallowing his pride uneasily. "I'm supposed to be a businessman, but every time I make a purchase, I lose money! It matters not if I'm buying or selling; it's as if I become enchanted and lose my grip and can't see right from wrong when the time comes to settle the business! My trading partners all get the better of me, and I'm always left short. What can I do to stop this vicious cycle?"

The prophet didn't waste precious time and immediately advised his friend: "When you see that you're being taken advantage of and are unable to make the proper decision, be patient and wait. In fact, try to wait for at least three whole days, for patience is one of God's most precious qualities, while rushing headlong into decisions is specific to the devil!" He then continued: "When you throw a slice of bread in front of a hungry dog, does he eat it right away? Of course not! He first smells it to make sure it's safe, and then he eats it. The dog uses his power of smell to make wise decisions as they pertain to him, while men and women must use their minds and their wisdom!"

The prophet looked deep into his companion's eyes and knew at once that his advice had left its mark on the man's consciousness. He was reassured in his heart that his words would soon turn the man's fortunes.

Escaping the Fool

A young man was walking to work when someone unexpectedly whizzed by him with such great speed that he felt a rush of air brushing against his face. He turned around and saw Jesus of Nazareth running like the wind, prompting him to wonder whether a hungry lion was in hot pursuit. The man noticed that in fact no one was chasing Jesus, and he felt obliged to inform him. After a long sprint, when he had almost caught up with Jesus, he called out breathlessly: "Stop. Stop please! You're flying as fast as an eagle! But no one's following you!"

Jesus was in such a rush that he didn't hear a word. The man, though, did not give up and continued to chase him, screaming as loud as his lungs permitted: "For God's sake stop for a moment and tell me who you're fleeing! No enemy or wild beast is after you, so why this flight?"

"Don't stall me, I'm in a hurry to save myself!" confessed Jesus as they both continued to run side by side.

"Aren't you Jesus of Nazareth, who cures the blind and the deaf?" asked the man, looking perplexed.

"I am," asserted Jesus.

"Aren't you the prophet who sees the unseen, who breathes life into the dead?"

"Indeed, I am capable of all that."

"Isn't it you who can turn a lump of clay into a living bird?"

Again, Jesus admitted that he could indeed bring life to the lifeless.

"With your unrivaled gifts from the spirit world," continued the breathless man, "who would choose not to serve you?"

"As God is my witness, I whispered the sacred word entrusted to me by God to a blind man and a deaf man, and both were miraculously healed. I shouted the word at the mountain, and it shattered into millions of tiny little pebbles. I breathed the word onto a corpse, and he was given back life! But a thousand times I've wished it on the fool, and it's never had the slightest effect! That's who I'm fleeing to save my life!"

The Drummer Thief

It was pitch dark in the middle of the night, when silence normally rules, except tonight the unrelenting tap-tap-tap of a hammer and chisel made sleep a distant and unachievable dream. A fearless thief, who had managed to dodge the authorities, was patiently digging a crawl space under a garden wall, trying to get access to the house within. The house's owner, who had been ill for some time, lay sleepless on his bed tossing and turning in pain. The constant tapping guaranteed that he would find no rest.

Frustrated and misty in the head because of his fever, the owner forced himself to creep out of bed with great difficulty. He was intent on finding out the source of the uninterrupted and annoying noise. He opened the window and leaned out to see if he could spot anything suspicious in the dark.

"Who's there in the dead of the night?" he screamed, indeed expecting a response.

The tapping stopped momentarily but resumed at a greater speed in no time. The owner, much to his dismay, couldn't figure out where the noise came from or what its source could be! Once again, he shouted into the darkness: "Who's there? What're you doing making such a racket? Digging a well?"

"No, my friend," replied the sinister thief disdainfully, "I'm playing the drum for your pleasure!"

"But that's not the sound of a drum I hear!" replied the owner, confounded.

"You will tomorrow, when you hear the screaming and shouting of your household and that of your neighbors!" said the thief cunningly, implying that fools truly deserve what comes to them.

Dogs' Shelter in Winter

In wintertime, stray dogs find little food in fields, as the landscape is frozen. Every year, the dogs gather and tell each other that if they survive the freeze, next summer they must build themselves a shelter, because their undernourished bodies could never tolerate another harsh winter.

When summer arrives, the stray dogs begin to put on weight as food becomes ample in the meadows and they can eat to their hearts' delight. As they gain weight and become more robust, they convince themselves that no shelter would be large enough to contain their enormous, well-fed bodies.

In their hearts, they know better, and they try to stay focused on the hardship they endured in past winters and the certainty that it will recur the following year. But the dogs have become fat and lazy, able to convince themselves that no home will be capacious enough to shelter them from the cold. Thus, the vicious cycle is repeated.

Lover of Prayer

Songor was a Moslem slave who belonged to a wealthy master who happened to be a nonbeliever. The slave was a conscientious worker who was never at fault in performing his duties. He was always up at dawn and always the last to go to sleep, making sure that everything in his master's house was in perfect order.

One morning, the master woke up earlier than usual and decided to go to the public bathhouse before the crowds appeared. He went to Songor's room and, seeing that he was already awake, ordered him to collect the necessary items for bathing: a bowl to pour water over his body, a towel for drying, and a special mud block to scrub and wash his hair.

Having collected all they needed, the master and slave left for the bathhouse together. On the way, they came across a small mosque, and, as it was the morning prayer time, it was full of devoted Moslems. Songor, who was extremely fond of such devotions and prayed every chance he found, begged his master to allow him to enter the mosque and perform the morning prayers with his fellow Moslems.

"Master, I never get a chance to perform my morning prayers in the mosque; will you please allow me to do so now? I promise it won't take long. You can rest on this stool here until I'm finished."

The master was amenable to this delay but told him to be quick. Songor hurried inside the mosque and stood shoulder to shoulder with his brethren, performing his prayer. After it was over, the imam and all the men left the mosque one by one; soon the mosque was empty, except for Songor. The master waited patiently until the sun had risen and it was time for breakfast, but Songor was nowhere to be seen. Losing patience, he went to the entrance of the mosque and called for his slave.

"They're not letting me come out," replied Songor. "I know you're waiting outside, but please wait a bit longer, and I'll be with you in no time."

"But Songor, there's no one left inside the mosque! Who's not letting you out?"

"It's the one and only Allah! The same one who has bound your feet outside and won't let you come into the mosque, is holding me inside and not letting me go!"

Patience

The legendary physician Loghman had been in the service of the great king David for many years. During one particularly busy period when he was quite occupied with his numerous patients, he had been unable to pay his regular visits to the popular king of the Jews. After several weeks, when Loghman finally found himself free of patients, he decided to pay a call on his beloved master.

Duly he arrived at the palace and was told that David was busy at work in a nearby barn. As Loghman approached the ramshackle barn, he found David hard at work, with sparks flying in the air all around him. Immersed in the task at hand, David did not immediately notice Loghman enter the barn and continued toiling away. A heap of small metal rods lay before him, which he skillfully heated and looped into circles and then linked together, creating a smooth garment of chain mail. He continued in this fashion for some time, repeating the procedure patiently.

Until that day, Loghman had never witnessed the craft of manufacturing armor, and he was baffled. He was dying to ask David what he was making; however, he stopped himself and thought it best to wait and not interrupt the master craftsman. He knew that, invariably, patience directs people much more quickly to their desired objective, and he trusted his intuition. "When one doesn't persist in sating one's curiosity, one often gets what one wants that much quicker," he thought to himself.

Thus, Loghman remained silent and continued to patiently observe David. Once the king was finished with his work, he pulled the armor over his head and shoulders and turned to face Loghman: "This is the best outfit to wear at war! I guarantee that it will protect a man against the deadliest blows," declared David, noticing the surprise in Loghman's face.

Loghman was thrilled that he had kept his silence despite his curiosity and had not interrupted the master at work.

Balal's Passing

Everyone knew Balal and what a great man he had turned out to be, albeit only a slave. He had lived an honest life and had served his wonderful master with great love and respect. Balal had aged prematurely, but he didn't mind. As he lay on his deathbed, his wife could see that she was losing him fast.

"My precious love, you're leaving me!" she sobbed. "Misfortune is knocking at our door; we're doomed!"

"No, no my dearest!" uttered Balal weakly but compassionately. "It's time to rejoice and be merry! Until now, this life's been laden with sorrow and mourning. Let me tell you that death is in fact life itself!"

When Balal spoke of death, his face lit up like fresh tulips and narcissus, his eyes beaming with delight. One could not detect any sign of illness or the imminent death that awaited him, but these blessings were hidden from his wife, and she continued crying her heart out miserably.

"The time of separation is upon us!" she lamented.

"No, my love, the time for reunion has arrived!"

"You shall leave your family behind tonight and enter a strange and foreign abode."

"Tonight, I shall leave this alien place at last and step into my cherished eternal home!" uttered Balal as his whole being prepared for his final journey.

"Will I ever see you again after tonight?" whimpered his wife.

"I shall be among the great men of God! If you can keep your heart clear and aim for spirit, giving up your attachment to this lowly world, one day we shall meet again."

Balal spoke his final words with great love and warmth in his heart and closed his eyes for the last time.

Which City Is Best?

Two lovers had found a quiet corner in the rose garden early in the morning before the crowds appeared.

"My darling, you've traveled the world over and seen many beautiful cities and other incredible sites," murmured the young girl to her loved one, hoping to challenge him. "Tell me honestly, which is your favorite city?"

"There could only be one place in the world, my love, and that's right here! My garden of joy is to be by your side, even if we were in the middle of the driest desert! If I ever found myself at the bottom of a dark well but my love was next to me, I'd be in paradise! So the simple answer to your question is: the best city in the world is where one's love is! And for me, it's right here next to you."

The embrace that followed his confession was the sweetest either had ever tasted.

Guest Killer Mosque

Outside the town of Rey in Persia, there stood a mosque that had earned a shocking reputation. The town's inhabitants called it the Guest Killer Mosque, and for good reason! Strangers, however, did not know this deadly secret, and every time one arrived in Rey and took refuge in the mosque for the night, he was killed and his body recovered the next morning. People from Rey never entered the mosque at night, convinced that the place was haunted and that djinns lived in its dark, empty corners.

One day a man arrived who was well aware of the mosque's reputation but nevertheless wished to check the validity of the locals' superstition, as well as test his own courage. "I will not value my own body beyond its worth, for it's the spirit that's priceless beyond all," he argued to himself. "One's body will inevitably perish, but spirit is everlasting."

When the townsfolk found out about the stranger's intention, they unanimously tried to dissuade him. But, despite their best efforts, they failed.

"Dear concerned friends," argued the stranger, "I'm tired of this life and have no regrets. I yearn for a challenge; I don't mind the physical damage. To leave this world would be sweet for me, just like a bird who's been freed from his cage."

People tried to change his mind, reminding him of the tortuous pain that might be awaiting him in the mosque. They reasoned that to embark on a heroic course may at first seem like a simple choice, yet once fully engaged, the difficulties of the path will become all too clear; they told him that he'd be sorry. However, he turned a deaf ear to them. They pleaded with him to give up his crazy idea and not to tarnish the reputation of their town and its citizens any further with yet another murder. But he had no ears to heed their appeals.

"I'm not like a skittish housecat who buckles under at the first signs of fear! I've given up on my life. I'm afraid of nothing, and if I lose my life tonight, so be it; I've achieved my purpose," insisted the brave heart.

The townsfolk slowly began to disperse, realizing that their words were having no effect. Reluctantly, they prepared themselves to confront the man's

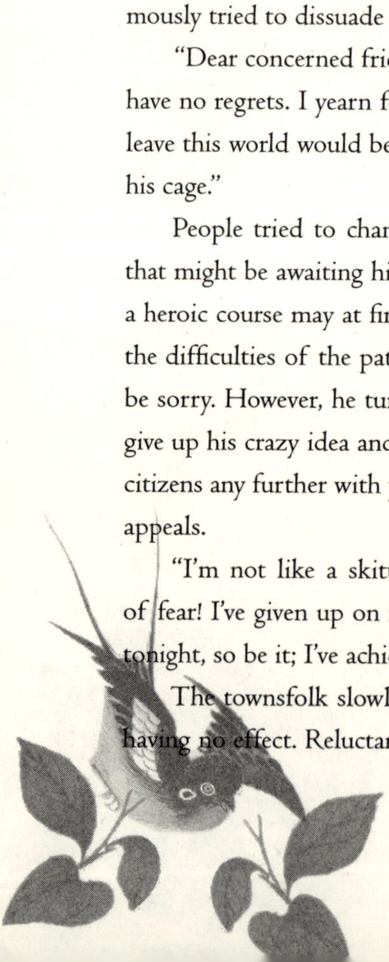

cold corpse the next day, and they each went their own way. Meanwhile, the man walked into the mosque, holding his head high against what might come. His head, however, had nevertheless been cluttered with the townspeople's warnings, and no matter how hard he tried he couldn't fall asleep. So, he sat in a corner, his back propped up against a pillar, and watched the darkness.

Midnight was upon him, and he had not yet heard or seen any monster or devil; he began to think that all he'd been told about the mosque had been lies or the product of the townsfolk's overspirited imaginations. Right at that very moment, he was jerked into reality by a piercing holler directed at him, declaring that in a blink of an eye his entire being would be overtaken. Any sane person would faint or collapse or even lurch into cardiac arrest, but not the fearless stranger, who had already bade farewell to his life on earth.

"This is nothing! It's the hollow sound of a drum declaring the arrival of Eid!" he shouted out confidently. "To the faithless, it may sound like the trumpet of death, but for those of us who believe in God, it's the sound of celebration! Why should I fear the drum of Eid? I shall enter the ring and either give up my life or leave victorious."

He got up from his corner and stood in the middle of the mosque, crying out: "Here I am! Can you see me? I've nothing to lose, I've given up everything. If you're brave enough, show your face and let's have it all out!"

With those words, the mosque's spell was broken; instantly, the ceiling cracked open and a stream of gold coins cascaded onto the mosaic floor. The man was stunned as he watched the unimaginable treasure pile up before him. After a few minutes, when he regained his composure, he ran about in search of empty sacks, which he found in one of the side rooms, and began to fill them up with the coins. It took him the rest of the night, but he managed to collect every single coin he could locate.

Unlike the cowards who had lost their lives in the Guest Killer Mosque, and much to the regret of the unbelieving townsfolk who had no trust in their hearts, the stranger became supremely rich, spending his wealth generously until his last living days.

Camel and Drummer Boy

In the Persian countryside, farmers used to teach their sons how to play the drums to scare away birds and other small animals that might otherwise threaten their crops. Young boys spent entire days and nights in the fields and played their drums to their hearts' delight. One of the drummer boys had been learning the skill since he was so small he could barely hold the instrument in his hands. He loved the sound as well as the motion of his fingers as he caressed the drum's skin. He also took delight in frightening the birds, especially when they all took flight simultaneously.

Sultan Mahmood, the ruler of the land, was quite fond of waging wars. He arrived with his massive army and set up camp close to the boy's family farm. Alongside the usual war-making equipment, the soldiers also brought a camel who carried their enormous war drum. The army's drummer thumped on the noisy instrument during times of war, day in and day out, without a break. Consequently, the camel was almost completely deaf and could hear nothing other than the sound of the great war drum. As the sultan's vast army spread its camp across the land, the camel happily strolled farther and farther away from his keeper, grazing on the fresh green grasses that he rarely had a chance to enjoy.

The morning after the army's arrival, the young farm boy left for work as usual, but a surprise awaited him—a camel, contently nibbling on his family's crops. He was quick to react. He picked up his drum and began to thump on it as hard and as fast as he could. On and on he drummed, and the sound carried for miles until everyone working in the fields could hear him. The camel, though, in its deafness, continued to calmly eat with great appetite, destroying the valuable crop of the boy's family.

When the boy's drumming had continued ceaselessly for hours, an exasperated farmer working nearby decided to walk over and find out the reason for all the clamor. When he found the boy and saw the camel close by, he figured out the problem. He walked over and knelt down beside the boy, putting his arm around the boy's weary shoulders.

"My young lad, are you drumming to scare away the camel?"

The boy nodded without interrupting his loud playing.

"You know that this camel belongs to the army, don't you?" the farmer asked.

The boy nodded again as he continued to play.

"Do you also know that he carries their enormous war drum? And have you seen the size of this drum?" The farmer spread his arms wide to replicate the breadth of the massive instrument. "This poor beast's ears are numb to the sound of your small, delicate drum, my dear. He probably hasn't heard a beat!" he told the boy gently. "Not every drum scares away every animal, and yours is not suited to drive away anything other than small birds and rabbits!"

The boy listened attentively and immediately stopped playing, realizing the futility of his effort. Silence finally spread over the fields, and the farmers could resume their work in peace.

The Chickpeas

On market day, a woman went shopping and came back with a big bag of chickpeas, which she intended to use to make several kinds of salad, dip, and soup. She cleaned the chickpeas, rinsing them well and then soaking them for several hours before boiling them slowly in a big cauldron.

As soon as the pot began to boil, the chickpeas started bouncing up and down, screaming: "You've bought us, we're yours, why set us on fire now?"

"It's time for you to boil, so stay quiet and be patient. I must cook you properly, until you're ready to be added to my best dishes," she asserted knowingly. "When you were growing in the fields you were amply nourished, but now it's time to put up with some hardship. You know that your ultimate purpose is to become nourishment for the spirit not just the body! That's how in the end you'll reap your greatest rewards."

The chickpeas slowly stopped bouncing around and quieted down, resigned to the fact that if they wanted to be part of the grand scheme of life, they would have to forfeit their material existence and trust in the guidance of their mistress.

The Mosquito and the Wind

It was the day of the week when Soleiman the prophet, who spoke the language of animals, customarily held court and heard the complaints of his subjects, whether they be man or beast. A mosquito had flown a long way to the city to see Soleiman and ask for his intervention to save his species.

"Great prophet, you are the most just ruler; you deal fairly and equally with every creature who comes to you, no matter if it's human, fairy, fish, or bird!" began the tiny mosquito. "I implore you to save us and grant us back our meadows and prairies. You solve everyone's problems, but you know how small and weak we mosquitoes are; in fact, we're renowned for it. While you're praised for your strength and greatness, we're unrivaled in our meekness. We're desperate for your positive judgment for us to survive."

"All right, little mosquito, whom are you complaining about?" Soleiman demanded. "Who's dared to injure you at a time when I'm still the ruler of this land? The day I was born, cruelty was ended! Mercilessness is rooted in the darkness of ignorance; when *my* sun is shining, how can darkness exist? I've been sent here by God to solve your problems so that you don't disturb Him every other minute. So, tell me, what seems to be *your* problem?"

"My complaint is directed at the wind! The wind is enduringly and irrevocably cruel to us, and we're fed up."

"All right, but God has ordered me to always listen to both sides of any argument. So I must ask the wind to be present as well to defend itself. It's God's rule, and I can't change it. So go and bring the wind back with you."

"But the wind is my enemy! Perhaps, would you be kind enough to summon it yourself?"

Soleiman beckoned the wind in the far distance: "The mosquito has a complaint about you; come forth quickly and defend yourself," he ordered.

The wind immediately changed direction and headed toward Soleiman's court. Straightaway, the mosquito made a move to disappear.

"Where are you off to?" Soleiman asked, surprised. "I must judge with both of you present."

"Great prophet, the wind's presence inevitably means my death! It's because of this wind that I have become homeless and destitute. That's why I came to you in the first place. There's only ever room for me, or for the wind!"

Before the wind entered the court of Soleiman, the mosquito had already flown miles away in the opposite direction, a little wiser about not challenging an opponent who's in an entirely different league.

MASNAVI IV

Praying Only for Sinners

In a remote town in Persia, there once lived a kind and respected holy man who was adored by everyone. However, there was a problem with him! He only prayed for criminals, murderers, and other sinners, beseeching:

> Oh God, the Benevolent!
> I implore You to never stop bestowing
> Your boundless compassion
> Upon the poor sinners of this world!

In his sermons, he almost never had kind words for those who were renowned for their charitable acts and had helped the poor and needy all their lives. One day, a group who attended his services regularly began to reproach him, telling him that his manner of prayer was uncommon and unappreciated by most of those present. The preacher responded to their complaint quite simply:

"Throughout my life, I've been the inadvertent recipient of many blessings because of the crimes committed by these unruly men. By the sheer evil of their actions, they've shown me right from wrong. Every single time I've turned my attention to worldly affairs, I've been witness to their immense cruelty; thus, I sought refuge in our Creator. Consequently, their evil actions have guided me to the greater good. It is imperative for me to pray for their salvation!"

People are forever complaining to God about their pains and the unfairness they experience in their lives. Meanwhile, God invariably tells His wailing subjects that it's that very same pain that will eventually lead them to His door. Our friends are indeed our worst enemies, for they remove us from His company by distracting us with the minutia of their own personal affairs. Truly, every enemy can be our cure and balm, for in order to avoid them we must seek the help of the One who has created us all.

The Most Difficult Thing in the World

Jesus of Nazareth was often presented with deeply profound queries from common people, and his answers frequently proved to be life changing for them. One day, an agitated man approached him hurriedly, waving to catch his attention.

"Please, great prophet, help me." The man panted heavily as he reached the place where Jesus had stopped. "What is the most difficult thing in the world to encounter?"

"God's wrath," Jesus replied instantly.

"How can we avoid it?"

"By suppressing *your* anger."

The man dropped his gaze and nodded gratefully. With no need to further explain the matter, seeing that the man had thoroughly grasped its essence, Jesus continued on to his destination.

The Sufi and His Cheating Wife

There was a Sufi who was a hard-working and honest shopkeeper who loved his wife; he felt that he would go to the ends of the earth for her. For some time, though, he had grown suspicious of her but was feeling guilty about his suspicions at the same time. One day he decided to go home earlier than usual. On that day, however, his beautiful wife had arranged for her lover to pay her a quick visit. When the Sufi opened the front door of his house, she was in the arms of the local peddler, lost in love and lust.

He slammed the door shut as he entered, barring any way out for a possible intruder. The lovers froze on the spot, unable to think of a way out. The Sufi, who possessed valuable foresight, decided not to make a scene and to maintain his wife's good reputation in the neighborhood, as he was still very much in love with her. While he was quickly strategizing an appropriate response, his cunning wife came up with a rescue plan. She quickly disguised the peddler under one of her veils, pretending that she was entertaining a visitor, in fact a woman inquiring on behalf of a suitor for their unmarried daughter.

The truth didn't escape the Sufi, but he had already made up his mind and decided to play along with his wife. "What service can we do for the revered lady?" he asked shrewdly.

"She's come to ask for our daughter's hand and would like to see her, but she's at school right now. The lady's son is a competent businessman but is out of town at the moment; that's why he's not accompanying her," the wife was quick to reply.

"It seems to me that this lady is grand and rich! Why would she want to marry her son to our poor daughter?" the man asked, feigning ignorance. "We're certainly not in the same class of society as her family! It's like building a doorframe with wood on one side and ivory on the other. When couples are not on the same social level, their marriage will not last long!" asserted the Sufi.

"I told her exactly the same thing, but she says that they have enough wealth to last them a few lifetimes and that what they're searching for is honesty and virtue in a girl, which are treasures both in this life and the next!"

"Well, she can see how destitute we are. Our daughter has no dowry, and her greatest asset is indeed her chastity and honesty, which is obvious to God and not dependent on my judgment!" he said, hoping that his words would be imprinted on the cheating partners' consciences without him having to disgrace them publicly.

The Tanner in the Perfume Bazaar

It had been a long, hot day, and the tanner had worked nonstop to finish all the orders he had received. As sunset approached, he felt more exhausted than usual; all he wanted was to go home, get a bite to eat, then lie down for an extended sleep. He locked up the tannery and began his long walk home, but as he was utterly drained, he uncharacteristically took a wrong turn and ended up in the perfume section of the bazaar.

As soon as he smelled the fragrant scents lingering in the air, his head went into a spin, and he passed out lifelessly on the floor. Passersby quickly gathered around, trying to help in any way they could. One rubbed his stomach gently while another sprinkled rose water on his face so that he would breathe in the heavenly scent. Someone else caressed his hands, while yet another rubbed his temples gently. A thoughtful shopkeeper quickly made him an infusion of various medicinal herbs, and his assistant helped remove the man's several layers of clothing. A concerned man took his pulse, while another smelled his breath for any sign of wine or hashish. Others stood around wondering how he could remain alive while looking so completely inanimate!

Eventually they discovered who he was and sent for his relatives. He had an astute brother who lived not far from the bazaar, and once he heard what had happened, he wasted no time getting to the scene. On the way, he quietly gathered a small heap of dog feces in the handkerchief that he always carried in his pocket. Arriving at the bazaar, he pushed folks away and managed to get to his brother's side while quietly reminding himself, "When one knows the illness, it's simple to find the cure! From dawn to dusk my brother labors in the tannery, surrounded by foul smells. When one falls ill, his only cure is that to which he's addicted. He's become sick because he's been exposed to the unfamiliar. His cure is dog shit not rose water!"

Unwilling to let the crowd discover what the actual cure was, the brother gently scattered the onlookers away from the supine tanner while

expertly drawing the handkerchief out of his sleeve and shoving it toward his brother's nose. As he bent over him, pretending to be whispering in his ear, he let him breath in the foul odor for a few minutes. Slowly, the tanner opened his eyes and began to move his limbs. People gasped in awe, thinking that the brother had used magic to bring the tanner back from the dead. Little did they know that the magic was nothing more than what the tanner was already quite used to—a foul stench!

Jump Off the Roof

Ali, the prophet's son-in-law and most trusted companion, was having a heated conversation with a Jewish man who did not believe in the Moslem God. Standing on a high rooftop overlooking the city, the Jew turned to face Ali and asked him: "Are you one hundred percent certain that your Allah irrevocably protects you at all times?"

"I've no doubt. In fact, I believe that I've been under His protection from the moment I was conceived in the womb!"

"If you want to prove to me that you have absolute faith in your God, then demonstrate that by jumping off this roof!"

"Be quiet," snapped Ali. "Before you choke on your words, you'd better stop! It's not for you or me to test God! We have no right to do so; it is only God who can test His servants, at any moment He chooses. Indeed, He tests us regularly to show us the extent of our devotion and faith."

The Jewish man had nothing more to say; he quietly left Ali's side and climbed down from the roof, pondering his *own* faith.

Mud Eaters

In the old times, there was a strange illness that had no apparent cause and no known cure, namely mud eating. People afflicted with this unfortunate condition could exercise no control over their behavior. Whenever they chanced upon even the smallest amount of mud, in whatever location, they couldn't stop themselves from scooping it into their mouths and swallowing it.

Mud eaters, however, also had to eat other foods to survive, and sugar cubes happened to be the favorite treat of one such afflicted person. One day, this man entered a small grocery shop in his neighborhood and asked the shopkeeper for a quarter kilo of sugar cubes. The shopkeeper, who was an astute businessman and knew about his customer's predicament, showed him the weights he used on his scale, secretly trying to tempt him.

"I use mud weights on my scale, just so you know! I'll be back in a jiffy," he said, inventing a reason to step out momentarily. "Give me a minute to fetch the whole sugar cone to chip your half kilo."

He turned around and went into the storage room at the back of the shop, making sure to take his time.

"This isn't simply mud!" the mud eater began to fantasize. "To me, this is more beautiful than any flower, more delicious than the finest pastry."

Delighted that the shopkeeper had left the room and hoping that he would take his time coming back, the mud eater eyed the weight delectably and snatched it in his fingers the moment he thought the other man couldn't see. He began to lick the clump of mud and nibble off small bites, savoring each one, no longer concerned about being caught in the act. He simply couldn't stop himself and no longer cared about risking his reputation. Meanwhile, the shopkeeper secretly watched his customer from behind a curtain.

"You're such a fool, you think you're cheating me, while you're only stealing from yourself!" the shopkeeper whispered silently to himself. "You're worried that I may reappear too quickly, before you've sated yourself, while I'm hoping that you eat your heart out! The more you eat, the less sugar I'll have to part with."

Even though each man was cheating the other, neither was aware that in fact they were cheating themselves, by being dishonest to a brother for the mere love of material.

The Darvish and the Firewood Gatherer

It was a cold and windy night, and a novice darvish had gone to bed early. In a dream, he found himself in the company of great Sufis and was quick to take advantage of his fortune. He implored the great men for advice on how to conduct his life honorably without creating bad karma. In their infinite wisdom, the masters imparted the great secret of the magical mountain, where fruit of all kinds grew on trees and one could subsist on them freely for life.

Without exerting much effort, the darvish soon found the mountain and discovered the delectable fruit of the trees, which were in abundance everywhere. Much to his surprise, the fruits were not only sweet but also transformed his speech in such a manner that when he spoke, people were mesmerized by him. He was content that he'd never have to worry about his livelihood again.

One day, the darvish went to a nearby stream to wash. As he took off his coat, he felt two silver coins that he had sewn into the hem of his jacket long ago while he was still a working man. Almost instantly he noticed an old man in the distance carrying a heap of firewood on his bent back walking toward him. He thought, as I no longer need the silver, why don't I give these coins to this poor man; perhaps he can nourish his dilapidated body a little. But before the darvish could finish his thought, the old man was standing before him, his eyes ablaze!

Unbeknown to the young darvish, the old man was a high Sufi master who could read thoughts. He threw his enormous stack of firewood in front of the darvish, inflicting the fear of God on him. Quietly the old man whispered something inaudible, but the darvish nevertheless understood him. He was reproaching the darvish for belittling him, thinking that he was so worthless as to be deserving of alms. The old man, obviously offended, raised his arms, turning to the sky:

"My God, only You know who Your special devotees are and what precious gifts they are to this world. So please, for our sake, use Your alchemy to turn this stack of wood into gold!"

Instantly the wood turned into pure gold, as if on fire! The young darvish was stunned; frozen on the spot, he was unable to move. After a while, the old man turned to the sky again: "O God Almighty, You are the all-knowing; for the sake of Your devoted servant, please turn this gold back to its original form."

The heap of gold instantly reverted to firewood, and the old man nimbly lifted the pieces onto his feeble back. He began walking toward the town, ignoring the calls of the young darvish, hoping that he had learned his lesson. He wished that the young man might remember this encounter and never again underestimate a working man's efforts to earn his keep rather than relying on handouts, like some.

Giving Up a Kingdom

Ibrahim, the ruler of Balkh, was wealthy and fair, admired by his people. One night as he slept soundly in his palace, he was awakened by thumping on the roof. He thought it might be his guards, chasing intruders who were running havoc. Before he opened his eyes, he thought: "Who'd dare try to enter my palace? Could it be a thief? But with all these soldiers and guards stationed all over the grounds, who'd risk his life?"

He angrily got out of bed and walked over to the window, thinking: "I hear the guards giving chase, but no human would be foolish enough to try to steal anything from my palace! Surely they must be djinns," he concluded.

"Who's out there in the dark of the night?" he screamed out the window, as loudly and ferociously as he could.

"It's us," a group of men yelled back in unison.

"What are you looking for?" inquired Ibrahim, confounded.

"We're chasing camels!" they said matter-of-factly.

"What idiots! Why would anyone chase camels on a rooftop?"

"For the same reason that you're chasing God while lying in bed!" they rationalized. "Is what we're doing so much more incredible than what you're doing?"

When Ibrahim heard those words, he gasped in awe, reached for the first outfit of clothing he could lay his hands on, and left his palace for good. No one ever saw him in the province of Khorasan ever again. His name, as a great Sufi, became renowned throughout Persia, and his story was told and retold for years to come, inspiring visions of the mysteries of the spirit world.

Darvish in the Garden

It was a beautiful sunny morning, and a darvish left home early intending to run a few overdue errands. Soon he found himself walking past a lush garden filled with fragrant roses and amazing, plentiful fruit trees. Instinctively, he entered the garden, intending to spend a few quiet moments alone and meditate on the beauty he had just witnessed. He found a secluded corner and sat down, making himself comfortable on a bench in the midst of the shrubs. Resting his head on his knee, he began to contemplate the grace of God.

A young man, who had also been mesmerized by the beauty of the garden, walked past the darvish and thought that he had fallen asleep. He couldn't hold his tongue and without any consideration for the man's privacy approached him and began a soliloquy, accusing the darvish of shutting himself off from the magnificence that God had created.

"It's a crime when you refuse to take advantage of the blessings that God has provided us with," the young man asserted aggressively. "What are you doing closing your eyes to all this beauty that surrounds you? By not taking advantage of it, you're in fact committing an unpardonable sin!" he continued, self-pleasingly.

The darvish slowly raised his head and knowingly gazed at the intruder as he rambled on but kept his silence until the young man finally fell silent.

"The signs of the Beloved, young man, are imprinted on one's heart, and that's where you should seek them," the darvish began. "The beauties that you speak of exist only in the outside world, while within my heart there's no limit to God's glory. The trees, the flowers, and the fruit that you see are only *signs* of His creation; they're merely a reflection on the surface of the water," he said softly but assertively, lowering his head again onto his knee and shutting his eyes as he resumed his meditation, ignoring the intruder's presence altogether.

Silence Is the Reply to Fools

At the king's court, there were many obedient and hardworking servants, except one. Unlike the others, this servant was lazy and greedy, unable to ever finish any task assigned to him. One day the king, who up to then had been extremely tolerant, finally got fed up with the servant's stupidity and ordered the treasurer to reduce his salary drastically.

Soon it was payday, and all the servants were enthusiastically awaiting their wages. When the stupid servant was handed his reduced amount of money, he couldn't believe his eyes and flew into a fury. Instead of finding out why he had been admonished, he began to curse and blame the cook for slandering him. The cook, who had been the one to hand him his reduced wages, told him that he was innocent and only the messenger. "If you truly want to find the real reason for your punishment, why don't you take a look at your own behavior? You'll soon discover who's the real culprit," he advised the servant.

The servant, however, turned a deaf ear to this good advice and sat down to write a letter of complaint to the king. He began the letter by praising the king, but his vicious tone did not go unnoticed. The king in his infinite wisdom chose to ignore the letter altogether.

When the servant never received a reply, he became suspicious of the messenger to whom he had entrusted his letter and thought that he had betrayed him. Soon again, he flew into a rage and cursed the messenger, making an even greater fool of himself than before. Unwilling to give up, he wrote more letters to the king each week, all of which went unacknowledged. After several months, one of the king's emissaries who was familiar with the case pleaded with the king to respond to his servant and release him from his self-inflicted torture.

"To respond to him is easy for me and to forgive him his laziness and stupidity, even easier," replied the king wisely. "Yet I choose not to infest the other servants with the same ailments that he suffers from, namely weakness of character and absence of intelligence. Therefore, I say to thee, the answer to fools is silence!"

The Large Turban

The size of a turban in the old days was indicative of a man's valor and stature in his society. In one small town, there was a middle-aged teacher who didn't have a bean to his name and went hungry most days, but he was too proud to admit his destitution to his associates. He regularly collected scraps from fabric shops, discarded wads of cotton, and cut-off pieces of people's unwanted cloaks, stuffing them into his modest turban to make it look more substantial. With time, his old and dirty turban came to resemble a sultan's silk headdress, fooling everyone in school and buying him much respect in town.

His students never thought for a moment that their revered master was not who he pretended to be, and the townsfolk didn't have a clue that when they bowed to his apparent opulence in the street, they were honoring an imposter. Only he knew that his good reputation was based on false pretenses—that, in fact, it was nothing but a big lie.

One early morning before sunrise, the teacher left his home and began his daily walk to school, preparing the morning lesson in his head. Unbeknown to him, a lowly thief was hiding behind a pillar around the corner, waiting for his chance. As soon as he caught site of the oversized, ornate headdress of the teacher, he thought that his opportune moment had arrived. It was well known among thieves that people of means generally hid their money and jewels in their turbans to keep them out of plain sight.

The thief waited patiently, confident that he could easily overcome the scrawny man coming his way and eagerly anticipated his moment of victory. As the teacher approached, in the blink of an eye the thief knocked the turban off his head, picked it up swiftly, and ran off with it. The teacher was confused at first and couldn't gain his bearings, but soon he realized what had happened and then chased after the thief.

"You good-for-nothing!" he screamed after him. "Look inside that turban first before you rejoice! You'll soon find out what you've achieved! Nothing! There's absolutely nothing worthwhile inside!" he loudly confessed.

The thief stopped running and pulled the turban apart to find that indeed nothing was inside but useless pieces of discarded cloth. He threw the whole lot onto the ground, losing his temper and cursing both the teacher and his sorry luck.

Intelligence

A young man was in trouble. He faced a dire problem that was consuming his life, making him miserable company for everyone he knew. Hard as he tried, he couldn't figure out how to free himself from the web that he had, through his own behavior, spun and entangled himself in. He took endless walks and spent hours on end in different teashops and coffee houses, engaging with strangers, seeking advice. Despite his efforts, however, his problem seemed unsolvable.

One day, he entered a particular coffee house for the first time and saw an older man sitting quietly in a corner. He recognized him immediately but didn't approach him right away. Instead, he sat at a table where he could keep the man's profile in view. He studied the older man with interest, remembering him as highly intelligent and a fair judge of character. After a few long minutes, he mustered his courage and walked over to the man's table, asking if he could sit down for just a minute. The man looked up from his book but did not seem very pleased at this interruption. He nevertheless nodded, and the young man quickly sat down and immediately posed his query. The older man was taken aback at the younger one's candor and shook his head thoughtfully.

"My good man, you must seek the advice of someone else, someone who's your friend. I'm your staunch enemy and will only misguide you. Why would you want my advice? You need a compassionate ear, one who only wants the best for you. You can be certain that you've no need for any words of advice I may have!" he suggested honestly. "If you were sitting in the midst of fire but had a friend with you, you'd think you were in a rose garden! And if you were in the middle of the most heavenly garden but were in the company of enemies, you'd feel like you were at the epicenter of a bonfire! So go on and find a counselor who's your true friend."

The older man had spoken his truth, hoping that his advice had not fallen on deaf ears and that he would be left alone in peace now.

"I am well aware of your feelings toward me, sir," admitted the younger man. "But I'm also aware that you're a highly intelligent person and would never commit a wrong deed. You would, therefore, never advise another person to do so either; that's why I trust your judgment far above my own or any friend's."

Leadership

In the first years, after the prophet Mohammad had originally introduced Islam to the people of Arabia, he was forced to wage many wars to firmly establish his nascent religion. Having fought in many of the battles himself, he was well aware of the importance of a competent leader. The time had come for yet another war, and he needed an able general. The prophet looked hard at his options and came to a final decision. His choice to lead his army was a young soldier who had not only fought exceptionally well but had also shown impeccable wisdom in making quick and wise decisions during battle.

Once the prophet announced his decision, one of his older companions, unable to control his anger and jealousy, approached Mohammad to complain. He simply could not accept taking orders from a younger man.

"You're our great messenger," he said gravely. "I beg you to reconsider your choice and refrain from selecting this young man! Didn't you always say that leadership belongs to the elders? We've several older soldiers who are far more deserving of this position. Don't look down on the yellow leaves of trees. Remember, they symbolize maturity and are responsible for producing ripe fruit in the end, while green shoots only signify youth and inexperience. An older person may have a tired body, but his intelligence is incomparably deeper than a young person's."

The man continued with his soliloquy, annoying the prophet more acutely with each passing moment. The prophet tolerated the older man's complaints for as long as he could but eventually cut him off and tried to reason with him.

"You only see the obvious and are blind to this young man's superior hidden qualities!" he asserted. "There are many men whose beards have not yet turned white but possess unrivaled qualities that their elders can only dream of. Likewise, there are many older men with long, white, distinguished beards whose hearts are tainted with unforgiveable sins. A commander must be intelligent; what does he want with a white beard? Isn't Iblis, our very own devil, the oldest man in the world? When one doesn't have a good mind, one has

nothing! Only the shortsighted consider white hair by itself to be a sign of maturity. My dear companion, strive to detect the essence of things so you may take command of both your faith and your mind. A wise man possesses an innate light with which he's able to guide and lead others; and I'm convinced that this young man has exactly that!"

Mohammad could easily have continued with his discourse but thought better of it and stopped. He hoped that his words had penetrated the old man's heart and mind with sufficient gravity so that he would never again have to counter any soldier's biased remarks, which could cast doubt among the entire army.

Three Fish

In a small pond at the foot of a mountain, where the water was as clear as the first drops of a spring rainfall, there lived three incredibly beautiful fish. They had swum in the pond all their lives and had never been disturbed by predators, until one day a few men happened to walk by and spotted them.

The men quickly rummaged through their packs trying to find anything they could use to catch the fish. Soon they found an old fishing net, all tangled up, among their normally useless bits and bobs. The three fish watched the men as they hurried about their business noisily but didn't guess their intention and continued swimming around calmly.

One of the fish, however, who was more intelligent than the other two, became suspicious and thought it best to leave the pond as soon as possible, without confiding in his friends. He reasoned that if he shared his intention with the other two, they'd try to dissuade him, as they were excessively attached to their home and old ways and might be unwilling to give them up. He had made up his mind, though, and was prepared to bear the consequences to save himself from what appeared to be their imminent demise.

Without further delay, the wise fish took a leap and braved the fast current that flowed out from the pond, following a stream that ultimately poured into a vast sea, the opposite shore too far distant to be visible. Once he found himself in the warm waters of the sea, he felt free at last; he could swim endlessly without having to circle around time and time again, like in a fishbowl. His new life was good, and he was thrilled that he had believed in himself and taken a chance on the unknown.

Meanwhile, the men continued to untangle their net, preparing to cast it into the pond. The second fish realized that she had wasted precious time and that her luck might have run out, so she began to conjure up an escape route as fast as she could. Initially, she blamed herself for not having followed her wise friend, who was now probably swimming free in the ample sea. Quickly, though, she stopped herself from dwelling on her mistake, as she knew that when the past is gone, it's gone! She could think of no plan of escape other

than pretending to be dead. So she rolled onto her back and, with her belly facing up toward the sky, floated on the surface of the water weightlessly.

The compliant water carried the seemingly dead fish gently on its ripples, up and down and around the pond. When the men saw the dead fish, they comforted each other that, although it was a shame to lose one, they should be grateful that they'd been spared dealing with a sick fish that was going to die anyway as soon as caught. One of the men grabbed the tail of the apparently dead fish as she floated on her back in front of him and threw her onto dry land. Without delay, the suddenly resurgent fish gathered all her might and flipped over and over behind the men's backs until she finally found her way to the fast-moving stream that eventually took her to the salty sea. Free at last, she swam with all her strength to get as far away as possible from the shore, hoping to never again lay eyes on another human being.

The third fish, however, was stupid. In a frenzy, he flopped around and around in circles, hoping to evade his captors as they watched from the bank. He proved easy to catch, however; the men simply threw their net over him and in no time had him roasting on a fire. Unbeknown to the men, while burning inside out, the fish kept repeating to himself, knowing well that it was much too late for regrets: "If I could have a next time, I'd pay closer attention to my wise friends and aim for the sea, which I'd make my home and forsake this lonesome pond forever."

I Am God

Bayazid of Bastam was a supreme Sufi master with many followers and devotees. He was famous for his seemingly mad utterances, which erupted from him when he went into trance. Those who knew him well and loved him unconditionally were familiar with his unusual states of mind and turned a blind eye to his peculiarities, letting him exaggerate as much as he liked.

One fine spring day Bayazid was in the company of his favorite students and felt exceptionally jolly, impatient to begin the *sama*. Often while he whirled, he would experience highly charged states of mind, shrieking and repeating words that were incomprehensible to the others present. That day, his followers noticed that he was overexcited and that his actions were especially unusual. His mood was also somehow different from the other times when he became engrossed in spiritual rituals; nevertheless, they didn't allow themselves to become concerned.

The *sama* started with the familiar sound of the reed, and before long Bayazid went into his trance as he whirled. "I am God!" he began to shout. "And there's no other God but me!"

His devotees were flabbergasted, not knowing what to make of their master; for this was the first time they'd heard him uttering such unmistakably blasphemous words. However, already accustomed to his frequently unusual behavior, they didn't think too much of it. The next morning, though, they told Bayazid what he'd said the previous evening.

"If I ever utter those words again, you have my permission to stab me repeatedly," he ordered. "In fact, kill me on the spot!"

The murids took Bayazid's words literally, and each decided to carry a knife in his belt at all times, just in case. The following week, they all gathered for yet another session of *sama*. Bayazid, as usual, became entirely overcome with excitement and began to whirl speedily, forgetting his instructions to his devotees of the week before. Soon he was in an exceptional trance and began to repeat: "I am God, I am God."

This time, his enthusiasm had no limits; the broad implications of his words rose to another level. Round and round he whirled, loudly praying all the while. "Under my shirt, lives God!" Bayazid shouted. "Why do you search for him on the earth or even in the sky?"

The devotees found themselves at an impasse; they didn't want to stab their shaykh, yet they didn't want to disobey him either. Eventually, one by one, they pounced on Bayazid and began to thrust their daggers toward his body. One murid aimed for his throat to shut him up, while another went for his heart, and yet another plunged his dagger toward Bayazid's side, trying to make sure that the man was as good as dead.

However, an odd sort of miracle occurred. With each forward thrust, the knife inexplicably spun around and stabbed the devotee instead of Bayazid. Each attempted blow at the master became an even more severe wound suffered by the murid wielding the knife, and in a few short minutes corpses piled around the room. There were a few men present who, despite their master's earlier order, had not had the heart to stab him. They stood by in a state of utter bewilderment, their tongues tied, watching the massacre! Their faith and trust in their shaykh, and perhaps the softness of their hearts, were what saved them.

From that day on, people from faraway lands would come to sit at the foot of Bayazid, to be in the presence of God.

The Bird's Advice

A beautiful bird was chirping happily on a branch when, all of a sudden, she felt a heavy cloud pressing her down to the ground. A cunning huntsman had managed to trap the stunning little bird in a net. Flapping around, she was unable to free herself from the man's snare. Quickly she assessed her dire situation and came up with a clever solution. She pleaded with her captor:

"O great hunter, you must have captured many impressive beasts in your time and feasted on innumerable cows, sheep, and other delicious animals. Yet none of them seem to have appeased your hunger. Let me assure you that neither will my tiny body with its minuscule amount of flesh. Allow me to offer you three pieces of advice that are far more valuable than my worth as simple prey."

The hunter was unsure of the bird's intention and whether he could trust her. The little bird felt his uncertainty and was quick to add:

"I assure you that you will reap infinite riches using these three precious bits of advice. I will give you the first counsel while still in your grip, and if you like it, then I will tell you the second one from the roof of your hut. The third and most important one I will impart to you from that tree," she said as she pointed with her beak toward a nearby poplar.

The hunter was still not convinced but reluctantly agreed as he saw that, truly, the little bird was not enough to feed even one member of his large family. The bird, still in the man's grip, offered her first suggestion:

"My first advice to you, my good sir, is to never believe the impossible from anyone."

The hunter kept his word and released the little bird, who flew to the rooftop.

"The second advice is to never regret the past. When something is in the past, it's never coming back."

The man, waiting to hear the third piece of advice, watched the bird as she flew to the top of the tree.

"Inside my stomach, there's a rare pearl that weighs a hundred grams!" she said nonchalantly. "You've lost your only chance of ever owning it! Obviously, it wasn't meant for you; otherwise, you could have fed your entire family for the rest of their days."

As the hunter heard these words, he began to wail and sob like a woman in labor.

"Didn't I tell you to never regret the past?" the bird rebuked him. "Are you deaf, or did you simply not hear me? My other advice was to never believe the impossible. How could a pearl weighing a hundred grams be in my tiny body when I don't even weigh ten grams myself?"

The man pulled himself together and wiped the tears in his eyes, and sheepishly asked the bird for her third piece of advice.

"You've got to be mad to ask me for more!" exclaimed the bird. "Why would I impart a third secret when I've seen how poorly you've put the other two to use?"

She prepared to fly away, but before she did she called back to her captor:

"To impart advice to the foolish is like trying to grow crops in a salt field!"

Child on the Roof

A woman, beside herself with emotion, rushed into Imam Ali's modest home. Hardly able to breathe, she fell to her knees.

"O savior, I beg of you to help me!" she pleaded. "My one and only child has climbed onto the roof and gotten stuck in the gutter and will not come down, no matter how much I beg him. I'm frightened that he may fall, and I'll lose him forever. He's the light of my eyes, but he's too young to understand reason. I even pointed to my breasts so that maybe he'll climb down for milk, but he turned his face away."

Her tears prevented her from continuing as she choked on her words. Ali let her sob freely, conscious that her hysterical condition was not going to be helpful to her son. After a few long minutes, the woman calmed down. She looked up at Ali's kind face; he was watching her intently, his eyes filled with compassion.

"I'm at my wit's end, my lord," the woman whined. "Tell me what to do."

"Now that you've calmed down, my good woman, listen carefully," Ali began softly. "Go and find another child nearly the same age as your son and send him up to the roof. When your son sees the other boy, in whom he will see a resemblance to himself, he will walk over to him. I promise you, like prefers like. We're always attracted to those who are similar to us. Your boy will soon be safe."

The woman did not lose a beat and ran out the door in search of such a boy. In no time, her son was saved, voluntarily walking over to his new friend and climbing down the stairs together to safety.

The King and the Servant

The king was gripped with wrath at one of his servants who had committed an unforgivable mistake. He instinctively drew his sword to behead the poor man. No one in the court stepped forward to intermediate, as they all believed that the man's fate was now sealed. No one dared ask the king to forgive the young man, except Emadal-Molk.

When Emad, one of the king's most trusted and respected ministers, knelt before the ruler and asked for leniency for the servant, the king immediately withdrew his outthrust sword. He ordered the servant to retreat to his quarters and not to appear before him until his anger had subsided.

The servant, however, instead of thanking Emad for saving his life, began to act strangely after the incident. Like most others in the court, he had always adored Emad, but after the incident, he avoided the kind man. Soon, he even stopped greeting Emad when they crossed paths at court.

One day, a courtier asked the servant out of curiosity the reason for his odd behavior: "Why do you act so ungraciously toward someone who has literally saved your neck?"

"I didn't ask Emad to save my life!" retorted the servant. "My life doesn't belong to him to save! It belongs to the king, and he can take it or give it back when he chooses. In that instant when the king wanted to slash my throat, I was willing to give up my life. I wanted to become nothing before him. Ah," he sighed, "to have simply been nothing before that king of kings! But Emad took that chance away from me, and I shall never be able to regain that glory!"

Ants and Calligraphy

The ants left their colony late one morning and, uncharacteristically, took a left turn instead of continuing along their usual route straight ahead. Soon they found themselves walking on a white sheet of paper that someone was writing on. Astonished by the beauty of the script, a young ant, who could not see the fingers holding the pen, turned to the older ones and exclaimed: "Look at this beauty! See how breathtaking these incredible shapes are that this pen is creating! I never knew that forms could look so astonishing!"

An older ant, who had seen a little more of the world, replied knowingly: "This beauty is the work of the fingers that are holding the pen. The pen isn't the originator of this masterpiece, the hand is."

"You are both wrong!" a third ant interrupted. "This is the work of the arm. Just look at those skinny, bony fingers. How could they ever create such a chef d'oeuvre?"

Gradually more ants joined them, all eager to offer their opinions. Their leader, who was known for his superior intelligence, finally declared: "Don't believe that this work belongs to the realm of matter, because all matter vanishes with age like a dream. Material things are meant for physical life, but forms are originally created out of intelligence and spirit."

Unbeknown to even the wise leader, beyond intelligence and spirit, ultimately an act of God is necessary for anything to become manifest.

The Crow and the Grave

Cain had mercilessly killed his brother Abel and was carrying the corpse on his shoulders, unable to decide how and where to hide the body so he wouldn't be caught out by his parents, Adam and Eve. Never before had he been faced with such a daunting task, and now he felt lost. Looking around him as he bore the weight of the corpse, he tried to come up with a solution, but his mind was too limited to be of much use.

It was late, and the sky was turning dark; Cain felt that his chance to resolve the situation was rapidly disappearing, when he spotted a crow flying low toward him. At first, he thought it was a hallucination, but then as the crow flew closer, Cain could clearly see that he was carrying what seemed like a dead crow in his beak. Gracefully, the bird circled in the air, and just as gracefully he landed nearby. Slowly and gently, he let the dead crow roll out of his beak onto the ground, and he proceeded to dig into the earth with his powerful claws. Once the hole was deep enough, the crow used his beak to push the corpse in and began to cover the dead bird with the soil he had dug up only a few moments earlier.

Cain watched the crow in utter amazement, wondering how it was possible that a simple, common bird could be so much smarter than he was! Immediately he followed the bird's example and buried his slain brother in the ground, leaving no trace behind for his parents to ever stumble upon.

Unbeknown to Cain, people need guidance in almost all tasks they face on earth, and the simple crow had been assigned to teach this lowest of acts: grave digging.

MASNAVI V

The Famished Dog

An Arab man was hunched over by the side of the road next to a dying dog, weeping grievously. Another Arab walked by and saw him.

"Why are you wailing like this?" he asked empathetically.

"I'm grief stricken for my dog," replied the sobbing man. "He was an excellent companion, but he's dying now. He fetched my food in the daytime and guarded my home at night. He had a quick eye and was a fierce hunter, scaring away any thief who dared approach our home."

"What's his problem now? Is he injured?"

"No, his problem is hunger!" confessed the owner. "He's so hungry that he can't move anymore."

"May God grant you patience. May you find another worthy dog like this one again," commiserated the passerby.

The two men watched the poor dog as he continued to pant and whimper. The passerby suddenly noticed a large bag next to the Arab's foot and asked him: "What's in the bag?"

"Oh, nothing much, just the leftover food from my meal last night. I'm taking it home so it can nourish my body again tonight."

"You must have some dry bread in there. Why don't you give it to the poor dog?"

"Hold on, I don't have *that* much affection for him!" replied the Arab, sounding quite surprised. "I find it hard to part with anything before I get paid for it first. But then again, tears are free!"

"What kind of a human being are you?" exclaimed the man. "The place for you is in hell itself! How could you even begin to imagine that a loaf of bread is more valuable than a single teardrop? Don't you know that our tears are the sorrows of our heart manifested into visible drops?"

The owner of the dog watched the other Arab walk away shaking his head in disbelief but sadly could not comprehend the magical piece of wisdom he had just been offered.

Peacock

A physician was taking a walk one day in the lush meadows behind his home when he spotted a beautiful male peacock in the distance. Curious to see the peacock up close, he carefully made his way toward the bird. Squinting his eyes to focus better and make sure he wasn't mistaken, the man saw that the bird was cruelly pulling out his sublime feathers with his beak and spitting them as far away from himself as he could. The man was perplexed and decided to investigate, so slowly he approached the bird.

"Hello, heavenly creature! What are you doing pulling out those exquisite feathers of yours?" he asked softly, keeping his voice low but unable to hide his concern. "How can you accept in your heart to destroy such beauty? Your feathers are admired around the world. Those who memorize the Koran use them as bookmarks, and noblemen use them to fan themselves in hot weather. Are you aware who it was that created your unrivalled glory? How can you throw away God's gift so ungraciously?"

As the wise man spoke his mind, hoping that the peacock had a good listening ear, he realized that perhaps he had been too rash in questioning the bird in the first place. Perhaps he had also been too quick to offer his advice; every activity has its own designated time and place, and he had not respected this fundamental reality. Nevertheless, he could hardly conceal his anguish as he watched the bird continue his plucking.

"Get away from me," exclaimed the peacock, clearly annoyed. "You're still distracted by my superficial beauty! Can't you see that it's because of these feathers that I've had to bear so much pain? Every time I turn around, there's a hunter stalking me. I can't protect myself from harm; I'm large in size, but truly I'm quite weak. If I can't repel danger, then I may as well make myself look as unseemly as possible! I want to be able to roam anywhere I choose, peacefully and without fear. These feathers are the cause of my egotism, they've brought me much unnecessary harm. It's time for me to be rid of all such ornaments! If anyone can understand, it's God!"

The peacock resumed plucking the remaining feathers, ignoring the man, who continued to stand by watching in silence as his tears flowed uncontrollably.

The Ready Lover

A young couple had fallen in love but, due to unforeseen circumstances, had lost touch with each other for almost a year. Not having spoken a word the entire time, they were almost at the end of their tether when one day, by chance, they came face to face in a rose garden.

"My darling, I can't believe my eyes!" gasped the boy, almost out of breath. "I've been heartbroken and lost without you. Life's been nothing but hell; my tears have dried up altogether. I've endured more hardship than I can fathom."

He went on and on without letting the girl utter a single word. He was so engrossed in his story of self-pity that his eyes glistened with selfish tears! The girl listened to him patiently until she found an opportunity to speak.

"You've done everything, my dear, except the main thing," she told him sadly.

"What could that possibly be?" asked the young man, flabbergasted.

"You've clutched vainly at issues that are only secondary and given up on the main issue, which is understanding the essence of love!"

"What's the essence of love?" he asked, confused.

"Nothingness!"

"Nothingness?" the boy blurted out, even more confused.

"Yes, my dear, you did everything you thought was proper, believing that's what lovers must do. But you forgot that you must be ready to die for your love. You're still alive, and very much so. If you're a true lover, then die right here before me so I know that you believe you must give up your entire being for your love."

When the young man heard his beloved's words, he quietly lay down before her feet, closed his eyes, and simply expired, bearing a wide, contented smile on his young lips as he passed from this life.

Tears during Prayer

One of the five pillars of Islam is prayer—done five times a day—and nothing must interfere with praying. The words spoken in prayer are the Moslem's tools for connecting with God and are paramount to one's existence. It's imperative, during the prayer, that one's mind doesn't drift off and entertain thoughts other than the words of the prayer itself.

One day a man went to his mufti and asked him: "Are tears allowed during prayer?"

"Depends on the tears, my good man," replied the mufti.

"How so?"

"If the tears have their source in the spiritual world—if they've sprung forth because of a spiritual experience and one's established a connection with the divine—then tears are a grace! However, if they've sprung from some physical pain or emotional discomfort, then they're a distraction and indeed may cut off one's connection with God; such tears are certainly not welcome."

The Moslem had his answer, thanked the mufti graciously, and left for the mosque.

Charity

In Zarvan, a beautiful and quiet village in Yemen, there lived a pious man who was a prosperous farmer. He was blessed with a most pleasant demeanor and a kind heart. He was also the fairest and most generous man in the village. Whatever he generated, whether a good crop or a profitable business transaction, he always contributed one-fifth of it to the poor, as Islam decreed. He never failed to remember, though, who was the ultimate provider of his wealth.

The farmer's home, because of his charity and benevolence, had become a safe house for many who were down on their luck. Penniless Sufi darvishes lived there from time to time, as well as travelers who had nowhere else to stay when they passed through Zarvan; additionally, the village's poorest residents would come and go regularly when they were in need.

The farmer was famous in the region; people knew that he always separated out what he intended to distribute to the poor from what he himself would take home for his personal needs. Out of every batch of wheat that he harvested, he put aside one-fifth of it for charity, and the bread he baked with it was always distributed among the needy. The farmer was sure that, come what may, he would maintain this altruistic routine until his dying day. However, he was not so sure about his children, whether they would follow his example. In fact, he was fairly certain that they wouldn't, seeing the way they looked at him whenever he distributed to the needy what they believed was their personal share of his wealth.

The farmer knew instinctively that what he gave away was not simply wealth flowing out the door but in fact a long-term investment. He believed that if one gave away the *zakat*, or one-fifth portion, of any gain, God would in turn guarantee a bountiful return. He was certain that sowing his seeds, tending to his fields and crops every year, and working hard at his livelihood were merely abilities that had been gifted to him, and that the true provider of life was only God.

He advised his children regularly to continue his ways, but he knew that they were against him and would never do as he wished. When it came to his children, he was merely sowing seeds in a salt field.

The farmer eventually passed away and, just as he had suspected, his children were uncharitable with the family's wealth and shut their door to the needy. Soon, their farms became unyielding and were left to rot, while the darvishes stopped passing through those parts entirely, keeping their blessed presence far from Zarvan and its people forever.

Majnoun

A great many love stories have been told through all time, but the story of Majnoun and his love for Laily is exceptionally renowned the world over.

Majnoun had fallen ill, and he knew exactly why: he had been separated from his beloved Laily far too long. The torture of not being in her presence had demoralized Majnoun, weakening his already frail body. He coughed incessantly and breathed only with great difficulty, unable to eat or drink. His friends eventually called a physician, who promised to do what he could to restore Majnoun to health. After thoroughly examining him, the physician announced that diphtheria had struck the lonesome lover.

"So, what's the solution?" the friends inquired impatiently.

"I know of no other treatment but to bleed him!" decreed the doctor. "Unless we rid him of the infected blood, he won't even survive the night." Immediately, the physician sent for the local bleeder, for this procedure needed an expert.

Majnoun, who had fallen into a semiconscious state, heard the physician's plan for treatment and made a great effort to sit up in his sickbed. The doctor tried to dissuade him from expending energy while attempting to lash down his arm with a strong piece of cloth, preparing him for the swift, razor-sharp cuts that would initiate the bleeding procedure, but Majnoun signaled that he wished to speak. "Leave me alone!" he yelled out as he shook his arm free.

"But my good man, you won't survive the night!" the physician tried to convince him.

"So be it! If my dilapidated body wishes to leave this earth, then that's what shall happen."

The friends, the bleeder, and the physician, who all knew that Majnoun had shown genuine courage in several escapades he'd been party to in the past, wondered if he'd now lost his nerve and was afraid to be cut.

"Majnoun," called out an old friend. "Since when are you afraid of a few tiny cuts? You, who I know has faced down wild beasts on several occasions in unknown lands, why be scared of this?"

"I'm not afraid of being cut; my entire body is in fact covered with love cuts," he responded dreamily. "I no longer exist, for my whole being has been taken over by my love for Laily. I'm simply afraid that if you cut me, you might be cutting her at the same time! Only those who are particularly sensitive can tell that there's no difference between Laily and me, that we're one and the same!"

Having spoken his mind, Majnoun turned his back on those who sought to help him and refused to be touched, instinctively protecting the love of his life, Laily.

The Water Carrier's Donkey

In the past, cities did not generally have running water, and therefore a water carrier would go from house to house to provide people with their daily water needs. In the capital city, there was an old water carrier who owned a donkey who'd pulled the man's water cart faithfully all his life. The poor beast's back had been bent in two because of the weight he had to carry every day, and his body was covered with untreated scabs and cuts.

His owner, not a great animal lover, did not feed the poor animal properly, because he could only afford old hay. The minute he mounted the donkey to make him walk faster, he'd beat him heartlessly with his whip, inflicting yet more wounds on the poor animal. The donkey, blessed with patience, obedience, and good temperament, wished every single day for God to take his life and free him from his constant suffering.

One day as they were doing their rounds, they bumped into the water carrier's old friend, who tended the sultan's stables. When the man saw the sorry state of the donkey, he was quite taken aback: "What's the matter with him? Why does he look so spent?"

"It's no fault of his," the owner was quick to reply. "He looks like this because I can't afford to feed him."

"Let me take him with me to the stables and tend to him. I'll feed him properly and let him revive a little," offered the friend generously.

The water carrier couldn't be happier with the offer and parted with his companion, hoping to pick him up the following week all plumped up and ready to serve him again. The donkey soon found himself tied up in the sultan's stables surrounded by beautiful, robust Arabian studs. When he realized what a great difference there was between himself and his new stablemates, he became disheartened and turned to God:

"Even if I'm a lowly donkey, I'm still one of Your creations! Why should there be such a difference between me and these other four-legged relatives of mine? Why should I suffer hunger all the time? Why should I endure pain all night long, able to sleep only fitfully, wishing every day that I were dead?

How is it fair that these horses should live in such luxury and I be demeaned to such misery?"

The donkey rambled on and on for quite some time, feeling utterly sorry for himself, when all of a sudden, he heard a loud trumpet blowing outside. A war had broken out, and the trumpet was announcing it. In the blink of an eye, soldiers amassed inside the stable and began saddling up the Arabians, who were in fact war horses. Soon, the donkey found himself all alone in the grand stable, wondering what had just happened.

The next morning, the horses stumbled back, covered with deep cuts and arrows still wedged in their flesh, their legs loosely bandaged. A team of veterinarians arrived on the scene; they tried their best to tend to the wounds, hoping not to cause more harm to the sultan's valuable steeds.

"Oh God, forgive me!" prayed the donkey, beside himself with embarrassment for his earlier self-pity. "I'm content with my poverty; at least I've got security! I'll gladly exchange the temporary comfort of these stables for my former despicable lifestyle any day!"

The donkey was relieved to be reunited the following week with his old, cruel owner, knowing now that nothing truly is as it seems.

Catching Donkeys

Pale as a sheet of thin paper, lips purple from fright, and shivering all over, a man hurled himself through the first unlocked gate he found in the alley. The owner of the house hurried into the yard when he heard the loud bang of the gate shutting and found his old acquaintance cowering in a corner.

"Greetings, my dear friend, what brings you here so early in the morning?"

The frightened man had not yet caught his breath and could hardly speak. The owner's curiosity was further aroused.

"What have you seen that has frightened you so?" he asked compassionately.

"The shameless king has ordered all donkeys in town to be confiscated!" replied the man.

"So? If they're catching donkeys, why are you running away? You're not an ass!"

"These men are very earnest and take their job seriously," he rationalized. "However, they're not experts and tend to make mistakes. I wouldn't be surprised if they were to get confused and nab the owner of the ass instead of the ass!"

The owner of the house stared at his friend in disbelief, not knowing how best to reply to such a comment.

Fear of Hunger

Sufi shaykhs, as a teaching method, would travel and take their *murids,* or students, with them, believing that traveling provided the best possible education. On one such trip, a shaykh and his murid were approaching a town that had fallen on hard times, ravaged by famine. The murid was young and inexperienced and had never faced a day of hunger in his life; therefore, he was apprehensive and focused only on the hardship that awaited him.

The shaykh was an experienced Sufi who had many years of practice in abstinence, so hunger and deprivation were hardly issues for him. Long ago he had overcome sensual attractions, and he was not going to allow thoughts of food to pollute his mind at this point in his life. Having a clear and pure mind, the shaykh could easily read his murid's obsessive thoughts and feel his fear of hunger.

When the murid was completely overwhelmed by fear and could no longer walk in a straight line, the shaykh turned to him and said: "I understand that the worry for bread has extinguished all your patience. You have given up on God and no longer believe that He will look after you!" he lamented. "But you must realize, to be hungry is to be one of God's special servants! Hunger is exclusive to God's favorites, and only *they* can experience it. You, my dear, don't belong to that special group, so rest assured that you shall never suffer for lack of food. God will make sure that there's always plenty to feed those who love their own stomachs, so don't trouble yourself worrying about your next meal!"

Having said his piece, the shaykh looked with pity at his murid, shook his head sadly, and continued to walk toward the famine-stricken town, wondering all the while whether his words had made any sense to the young man.

Cow on a Green Island

There is a green island that never dries up, forever spreading lush and bountiful. On this island lives a cow who feeds sumptuously on the grasses and grows fatter and healthier each day. All day long, he roams the abundant meadows and feeds without a moment's respite until dusk. Once darkness descends and the green can no longer be seen, the cow begins to fret.

"What am I going to eat tomorrow?" he agonizes. "Will there ever be any food to eat again?"

He worries himself literally thin! Every night, he loses all the weight he had put on during the previous day as he worries about the next day's provisions. In the morning, he's a mere shell of the cow he was the night before, looking lanky and unkempt. He can hardly walk straight from lack of strength and feels that it's his last day alive.

As the sun begins to shine and the greenery again becomes apparent, the cow cannot contain his joy. Without losing another moment, he pounces on the grasses, which have grown through the night until they now reach the underside of his belly, and eats as though he'd been famished for years. As he eats, he puts back on the weight that he'd lost during the night and soon becomes as fat and as strong as the day before. This cycle is repeated regularly; the cow frets all night and loses weight, and the next day, when he sees the grasses, he feeds on them and puts the weight back on.

"I spend my days grazing on this grass, but I lose all the goodness I gain from it in the nighttime, when I worry about not finding any grass to eat the next day," the cow occasionally ponders. "But every day there's plenty of fresh grass again for me to consume, and I do so happily. The supply never vanishes, but I don't seem to have any faith in it. I wonder why I behave this way—what kind of diseased thinking is this? What I gain during the day, I myself destroy in the night! Why can't I change? This has become my ingrained behavior, and there's nothing I can do about it."

While he's aware that he's taking the wrong approach to life, nevertheless the cow is unable to change. Habit has become so deeply implanted in his mind that there's no place for trust.

The Zoroastrian and the Moslem

Two men had been friends since childhood; one was a Moslem and the other a Zoroastrian. One day as they were drinking coffee, the Moslem turned to his friend and suggested: "My friend, how about you finally becoming a good Moslem?"

"If God wills it, I will convert," said the Zoroastrian cunningly.

"Allah wants you to turn to Him so that He can save you from hell, but it's your menacing ego that pulls you back toward disbelief."

"I know you as a fair man, my friend," replied the Zoroastrian gravely. "When that which you call the ego has conquered and continues to rule me, I've no choice but to obey it, for it is far more powerful than me. I would never dare think that anything in the world can be done without the will of God; therefore, I conclude that if He truly wanted me not to be a Zoroastrian, He wouldn't have made me one!

"If your Allah holds absolute supremacy and dominates all realms but still can't pull me toward Him, then His will does not exceed all. So, what's the use of me converting? He has bestowed free will on us, and we're responsible for putting it to good use, which I hope I'm doing!"

Having spoken his mind, the Zoroastrian continued to sit beside the Moslem, both quietly sipping their coffee in peace.

True Servitude

A destitute man was standing by the side of the road one day, hoping to receive alms from passersby, when he saw a group of men walking toward him dressed in colorful silk livery with brilliant, bejeweled belts. He had never seen people like these before and asked a person standing nearby: "Who might they be? Which kings and notables are they?"

"They're not kings or dignitaries; they're the servants of Omid of Khorasan, one of the sultan's ministers."

As soon as the poor man heard this, he turned to God in despair and let the words roll off his tongue: "God, why don't You, too, look after Your servants like Omid of Khorasan does?"

The poor man uttered these ungrateful words out of desperation, for he never had enough clothes to keep warm or enough food to stave off his chronic hunger. But not long after the incident, the sultan turned against Omid, accusing him of treachery, binding his arms and legs, and throwing him in prison. He ordered Omid's servants to be arrested, tortured, and interrogated until they divulged where Omid had hidden his treasure.

For an entire month, the innocent servants were tortured day and night. The frustrated tormentors threatened to cut out their tongues if they didn't reveal where the treasure was kept, but none of them spoke. In the end, the sultan became exasperated and ordered them to be killed. Their limbs were severed from their bodies, their tongues were cut out, and their corpses were thrown into a sewage-filled ditch outside town.

That very same night, when the poor man who had earlier cried out in despair at the wealth of Omid's servants was soundly asleep in the dark, damp entryway of a neighborhood mosque, he had a revealing dream. In his dream, a holy man approached him, saying: "This is a lesson for *you!* You must learn how to be a *true* servant, like Omid's men. Only then may you approach the door of God and be worthy of seeking His grace!"

Love Pulls the Ear

Majnoun and Laily's love affair was known to everyone, but some doubted its sincerity. One day, a group of suspecting men, whose vision was clearly constrained by their inferior intelligence, bumped into Majnoun as he wandered through the streets, his head filled with thoughts of Laily.

"Hello, Majnoun," one of the men called out. "We've been wondering about it for some time and can't figure out why you're so madly in love with Laily. She's no beauty—what do you see in her?"

Majnoun was caught off guard; his mind was totally occupied with thoughts of his beloved and couldn't exactly catch the men's train of thought. He looked at them with bafflement.

"Majnoun, don't look so surprised; we're serious! If you come with us, we'll introduce you to lots of beautiful girls, and you'll never look at Laily again!" another of the men boasted, quite pleased with himself.

"Your eyes are blind," Majnoun retorted. "You can never see her beauty! Not like I do! To only grasp what's on the surface is the reaction of an idiot!"

He turned to walk away but changed his mind and came back to the cluster of men.

"Let me tell you something," he asserted, his voice rising with each new phrase. "To only perceive what's visible to the eye is like having a beautiful jug but being oblivious to the real beauty of the wine inside, because you can only see the container. I drink from a pitcher, and I taste the delectable wine; but if you drink from the same vessel, God will only allow you to taste vinegar. Laily's love will never enter your hearts. Love for her shall never pull your ear. I'll taste honey from a pot while you'll taste poison. Every person sees what he chooses to see."

This time, Majnoun pushed his way straight through the group of men while holding his head high, more ecstatic in his love for Laily than ever before.

The Muezzin Caller

There was a town in the Levant where most of the inhabitants had not yet converted to Islam. In this town lived a muezzin caller who was cursed with the most exceptionally discordant voice. When he began the call to prayer, everyone in the vicinity fled so as not to be within earshot. The elders in the town were constantly pleading with the man to quit, believing that, instead of calling people to prayer, he might actually be scaring them away. Regardless, the man paid no heed to people's opinions. Every day, he climbed up the minaret and transmitted his ear-piercing call, sending people scurrying to shield themselves from the unbearable noise.

One early dawn, a well-dressed man holding a tray full of sweets and lit candles came to the center of the town and asked people how to find the muezzin. When people asked why, he said it was because the muezzin had brought much comfort and calm to his household.

"How could his awful voice bring comfort to *anyone*?" one townsperson asked.

"I have a beautiful, delicate daughter who's been wanting to convert to Islam for some time now," the well-dressed man replied. "We've been trying to dissuade her, but to no avail. It's as if love for Islam had penetrated her soul and sunk its roots firm and deep."

He took a long breath and gathered his composure, as he noticed that everyone was eager to hear his story and wanted him to continue. "I was devastated, knowing that if she changed her faith, we would lose her. I didn't want to lose my child but couldn't figure out what to do!"

"So, what made you look for the muezzin caller?" one onlooker asked impatiently.

"It wasn't until she heard the muezzin that everything changed!" he said with a grin on his face. "When she heard him for the first time, she was surprised, because she'd never heard such a horrible sound before. She couldn't believe that this noise was actually the Moslem call to prayer, so she asked her sister, who confirmed her worst doubts. But she still wasn't convinced and

asked several others, who all said the same thing. When she finally was forced to accept that this was indeed the prayer call, all the attraction she had felt for Islam vanished! She simply couldn't reconcile that the beautiful faith she had fallen in love with could include such an uncouth element. For the first time in ages I've been able to sleep soundly at night, and I owe it to the muezzin caller!"

The father then spotted the man himself, who was making his way to the mosque, and approached him, gratefully offering the gifts he had brought.

"At last you've put my mind to rest! You've given me back my daughter. If I were a wealthier man, I would lay greater treasure before your feet without a second thought. I'm forever indebted to you."

Having expressed his gratitude, the father gave the tray of sweets and candles to the muezzin caller and then hurried back home before the man could begin his abrasive call.

The Jester and the Chess Game

Seyyed Ajal,[4] the powerful ruler of the province of Termez, had a great love for the game of chess. One day, relaxing in his opulent palace, he summoned the court jester to set up the chessboard, as he fancied a challenge. Happy to comply, the jester eagerly prepared the board and sat before his master, ready to begin. Only a few minutes into the game, though, the jester suddenly jumped up and shouted, "Checkmate! Checkmate!" signaling that he had beaten the ruler at his favorite game.

Seyyed Ajal was a sore loser and did not appreciate being embarrassed. On this occasion, his anger got the better of him, and he began to hurl the chess pieces at the jester. "All right, you won!" he screamed. "Here's your reward, you lowlife good-for-nothing."

Seyyed Ajal cursed and threw every object within his reach at the poor, innocent jester, who begged for forgiveness. But soon the Seyyed's anger subsided and boredom got the better of him; he decided that he wanted another game and so beckoned the jester back. The frightened man approached the chessboard apprehensively but sat down to play. Once again, he beat his sovereign in a blink of any eye and had to call out the customary "Checkmate! Checkmate!" But before he did, he ran to an adjacent room and hid underneath several layers of bedding to save himself from Seyyed Ajal's anticipated blows.

"What are you doing? Why are you hiding?" asked the ruler, when he eventually located the jester.

"Checkmate! Checkmate! Checkmate!" called out the jester in fright. "While in your service, this is the only way I dare to announce my win, my lord!"

Such is the predicament of those who must live under unjust rulers with no respect for their subjects, whom they are supposed to be protecting.

4 The name "Seyyed" indicates a descendant of the prophet Mohammad.

Guest on a Rainy Night

It was a rainy night, and a traveler found himself stranded in an unfamiliar neighborhood. He had walked all day and was exhausted, hardly able to focus, yet he suddenly realized that the door in front of him looked familiar. He approached the house apprehensively and knocked gently, hoping that he was not mistaken. When an old friend indeed opened the door and invited him in warmly, his relief knew no bounds.

That evening down the street, the neighbors were having a circumcision party for their youngest son, and the owner of the house and his wife had been invited. Quietly, the couple decided between themselves that the husband should stay behind and catch up with his friend while she would go to the party. They also agreed that she should prepare the friend's bedding well apart from their own bedroom. The wife left the two men chatting away, reminiscing about the past as they sipped tea.

It was nearly midnight when the guest thanked his hospitable friend and went directly to the couple's bedroom, crept underneath the covers, and instantly fell asleep. The host, much too exhausted and far too embarrassed to wake his friend and tell him to change beds, snuck to the bed intended for their guest and also fell asleep immediately.

Not long past midnight, the wife returned from the party all jovial and excited. She quickly undressed and writhed her way underneath the covers next to the man she thought was her husband. She caressed and kissed him a few times and whispered in his ear: "My darling, I was so anxious that because of this horrid rain that seemed to never end, we'd be stuck with this man all night without a moment's peace."

The guest, now suddenly wide awake, heard her unkind words and, not losing another minute, sprang out of the bed furiously. "I have sturdy shoes and don't fear the rain or the mud!" he exclaimed. "I'm out of here! You keep your precious home for yourselves. A soul never rests while traveling!"

As he headed toward the door, the woman, feeling ashamed, grabbed for his legs and begged him to stay, hoping that he would change his mind and not leave her home with such animosity. But to no avail; it was too late for regrets. The husband also awoke during the commotion, and the couple watched the man as he walked into the darkness, his face illuminating the empty space before him and for miles ahead, like a ferociously burning candle. They could hear his voice in their heads, saying to them: "I am the prophet Kidr, and I have copious spiritual treasures to impart. I had intended to gift some of them to you, but it wasn't meant to be!"

The next day, the couple converted their home into a guesthouse, welcoming every traveler who came to their town, hoping that perhaps one more time the prophet Kidr might appear at their humble abode.

MASNAVI VI

Father's Will

A father loved his stunningly beautiful daughter deeply and held her in high regard. He also knew that she had to get married soon; otherwise, her reputation might suffer. He felt that he had to protect her against the fathomless jealousy of the town's women, so when the girl, still young, came of age, he agreed to marry her off. He bestowed her to a man whom he was not convinced was the best choice; the man was not of the same social class, nor was he financially in a superior position. But the father had made up his mind that the sooner the girl was married, the safer was her future.

"My darling daughter," he advised her, "I've no choice but to give you away to someone who's not of the same stature as you. You can't be sure of him, so it would be best to avoid getting pregnant for some time yet."

"Yes, sir, I'll do as you wish," the girl agreed obediently, trusting that her father knew best.

Because the newly married couple lived not far from the girl's father, he saw her often and never failed to repeat his advice every time they met; and the girl would show him her flat stomach to put his mind at rest. But then, one day, the girl became pregnant! She cunningly hid her condition from her father for a good six months until it was no longer possible to hide her bump.

"What is *this*?" scowled the father. "Didn't I tell you to keep well away from him? Or was my advice just some passing wind that never crossed your threshold?" The father was beside himself, knowing that his daughter no longer had a way out.

"Father, please," begged the girl. "You know that man and woman are like cotton and fire! How could I have avoided him forever? How was I to flee the fire?"

"I told you not to go to his bed!" the father bellowed. "And if he comes to you, make sure that he doesn't impregnate you! I told you to pull away when you thought he was at the height of his pleasure!"

"How am I supposed to know when he's about to peak?"

"When he becomes blurry eyed with a soft gaze, of course!" the father almost shrieked.

"But, father, before his eyes go soft, both of my eyes have already gone blind!"

The father knew well that his advice, albeit offered with what he thought were the best of intentions, was only so much hot air, blowing by gently and penetrating no one.

Poet in Aleppo

In bygone days, the people of Aleppo were mainly Shiite Moslems, and during the mourning month of Muharram, they held many heart-wrenching, tear-jerking, back- and chest-beating ceremonies. Men and women alike gathered every year at the city's Antioch Gate to mourn the brutal massacre of Hossein, the prophet's brave grandson, and his men by the cruel caliph Yazid. The eerie sound of the mourners' wailing could be heard well into the night, reaching far into the desert and rising to the skies in heaven.

One year, a poet had traveled to Aleppo on the night of the ceremony, the Ashura. When he heard the screams and mourning of the crowd, having no clue what was going on, he followed the sound to Antioch Gate to see for himself. When he saw the enormity of the gathering, he realized that the event must be for an exceptional figure.

"Who's this person whom you revere so much?" he inquired. "Tell me about him, for I'm a poet, and I'd like to write a poem in his honor!"

"Are you mad? You're obviously not a Shiite!" snapped one of the mourners with animosity. "How can you not know that today is the anniversary of the death of Hossein, one of the most cherished figures in our history? For a true Moslem, today is even more important than the day of Noah's storm."

"I do know about Ashura," the poet defended himself. "But the age of Yazid is long gone! How come you've only heard about this calamity now? Everyone else in the world has heard of this disaster, even the blind and the deaf. Has your lot been asleep all this time that you've only begun mourning for him now?" The poet was genuinely perplexed. The mourners, for their part, simply stared at the man, speechless.

"You're truly ignorant!" the poet finally blurted, again unable to hold back his tongue. "You should be crying for yourselves, because this deep slumber of yours is worse than death itself! Those holy men were the kings of their faith, and the day that their spirits separated from their bodies should be a day for rejoicing! Had you any idea of their true nature, you would have known that today, for them, is a day of joyous celebration. You should all be mourning your own dead hearts instead, for you've no consciousness except for this earthly existence!"

Without further delay, the poet gathered up his pen and paper and hastily rode out of Aleppo, wary that if he remained one more hour in this town, he might lose his faith in humankind and human intelligence altogether.

Tolerance

A young novice darvish had heard unending praise about the renowned shaykh Abol-Hassan of Kharaghan, and he could not wait to meet him. One day, he decided to take the long journey to the eastern province to fulfill his enduring wish. The journey was arduous, and it took him weeks to reach his destination. As soon as he arrived, he began to inquire about the shaykh's residence, and after hours of searching in the town's back alleys, he found the house at last. His heart was brimming with excitement and hope as he timidly knocked on the door, waiting patiently for it to open.

"Who's there?" came the sound of a woman's voice.

"Hello; I've come to pay my respects to the revered shaykh, ma'am. I've come all the way from Taleghan," he whimpered.

"What an idiot! You've endured such a grueling journey to this godforsaken town, and for what? Didn't you have anything better to do?" barked the woman. "What useless thoughts did you entertain in your empty head? Or perhaps it's the devil who's sent you here?"

There was no end to the woman's bickering. She went on and on, ridiculing and bad-mouthing the shaykh himself, trying her best to kill every hope in the young man's heart.

"Despite all, ma'am, can you please tell me where I can find the shaykh?" implored the murid, tears welling up in his eyes.

"So you're really looking for that charlatan, who plants lies in fools' hearts and ensnares them? He's trapped thousands of idiots like you already. You're better off never seeing him and going back home unharmed. Beware, he's a real charmer," she warned him. "A sorcerer must have tricked you into seeking out this goat who resembles a man, and you and everyone else like you worship him like buffoons. Stop caressing his ego; don't encourage him further. Go on and get out of here now."

The young Sufi couldn't believe his ears. He simply decided that the woman must be mad and that he need no longer bother with her incriminating description of his beloved spiritual master. He carefully backed out of the woman's view and decided to ask others about the shaykh's whereabouts.

But before he left, he couldn't help saying to the woman, whom he finally understood to be the shaykh's wife: "The light of your husband has reached East and West, yet you have no share of it. I will not return home because of your malicious words, and I will not give up my search for the shaykh. There are many bats like you who wish to smother the light of God, but I shall not fall for your false words. Farewell, and may God save your pitiful soul!"

Having vented some of his anger, the murid began asking everyone he came by for the shaykh's whereabouts. It took a while, but in the end one person was able to direct him to a nearby forest, where the shaykh was apparently gathering firewood. The young man hurried toward the woodland outside town while wondering why on earth the shaykh had married and remained married to such a vampire of a woman. He was baffled that two such opposite poles of the spectrum could live compatibly with each other.

However, he quickly extinguished this train of thought, as he felt that he was beginning to doubt the great man without knowing the full story. As he thus reasoned with himself, he suddenly saw an elderly man comfortably sitting on top of a heap of firewood that was in turn stacked on the back of a lion, using a huge snake as a whip to control the beast.

"Be careful, young man, to not let your thoughts wander too far from the truth," said the old man, having read the novice's mind.

By the time the shaykh reached the murid, he could construe exactly what had been exchanged between him and his wife, and he recounted the conversation to the young man, who listened in awe.

"I don't tolerate her behavior simply to satisfy my own ego," said the shaykh. "Had I less patience, how could I have tamed a lion? I'm not merely half-conscious of God's will, nor do I allow myself to be influenced by what people say or think. My entire being is under the command of the Almighty, and I give up my life gladly for Him. I don't tolerate her and others like her for worldly reasons; I put up with them so others may see how magnanimous my God has made me!"

Giving himself up completely to the will of his revered shaykh, the young murid felt his heart expand with light as he knelt before the great man and his obedient lion.

Camel, Bull, and Ram

For days, a starving camel, a bull, and a ram had roamed the prairie looking for anything green to eat, but they had not succeeded in finding a single morsel. The three kept each other company as they continued their search for food, hoping that by sticking to each other they might have a better chance. They searched under every rock and sniffed each dry bush that they thought might bear an edible surprise, until finally they found a small bit of wilting grass. They were overjoyed, hoping to feed their empty stomachs at last, albeit with a meager prize.

"This bit of grass is not going to suffice for the three of us if we share it. None of us will satisfy our hunger with this!" the ram said as he pointed toward the grass with his nose. "I've an idea though! Why don't we let the oldest of us feed on it, because respecting elders is a requirement in life. So let's each of us tell his age."

Immediately after he had announced his plan, the ram volunteered his age: "I'm the twin brother of the ram that the prophet Abraham sacrificed instead of his son, Ishmael."

"I'm the husband of the cow that Adam used to plough the fields after he was expelled from paradise!" said the bull in turn.

When the camel heard them lie so blatantly, he bent down and pulled out the grass with his mighty teeth. "It's obvious that being as tall and capable as I am, I've no need to be ancient like you to eat!" he said, not wasting another moment as he patiently chewed the delectable weed, teaching them both an invaluable lesson.

Treasure in Egypt

In Baghdad, there lived a man who had inherited great wealth. As he was young and inexperienced, he spent frivolously and was soon penniless. On the verge of becoming homeless, he turned to God, begging to be saved and to recover his wealth. He cried endlessly, feeling remorseful that he had wasted what had passed of his life and had nothing to show for it.

One day, having exhausted himself with many hours of lamenting and weeping, the young man fell asleep and had a dream. In his dream, a voice advised him to go to Egypt, where he was certain to find a great treasure that had been hidden for many years. What was keeping him, the voice persisted; why didn't he wake up and just go?

The man woke up in a strange mood, still trying to process the odd dream he'd just had. He thought, with nothing more to lose, why not join the first caravan that was headed for Egypt? And that's exactly what he did.

After several days, he arrived in Cairo, destitute, hungry, and unable to secure shelter. He was too embarrassed to beg openly, fearful even in this foreign city that he might bump into someone familiar from his more carefree days. Thus, he decided to wait for the cover of darkness before exposing his plight so that he could remain faceless. Although practically dying of hunger, he struggled with the humility of having to beg. Back and forth he went, undecided about how to approach people, and before he knew it, much of the night had passed.

The previous week, there had been a few robberies in the neighborhood where the man had ended up, and the police were on guard, having been reprimanded by the mayor for being too lenient on criminals. They were ordered to arrest anyone who might look suspicious, even if the detainee happened to be a relative of the caliph. The punishment for theft was nothing less than the amputation of one's arm! The police felt considerable pressure to find culprits, even if they weren't sure that a suspect was actually guilty.

When they saw the poor man from Baghdad cowering in a dark corner off the street and shivering in the cold night air, they were relentless and beat him mercilessly. The man cried out, begging them to allow him to explain why he was there, and finally one of the policemen took pity on him and stopped the others from beating him further.

"Go on, then, you've one minute to explain what you're doing out in the streets in the middle of the night! You don't look like you're from here. Tell me, what's your game?"

"I'm not a common thief," whimpered the man helplessly. "I don't go around robbing people. I'm from Baghdad and a stranger in your city."

Without further ado, the young man related his dream about the treasure; the policeman, detecting a hint of honesty in his story, felt sorry and kindly advised him: "I can see that you're not a thief or a criminal, but you're not very intelligent, are you? How could you come all this way just because of a dream you had?"

The poor man felt ashamed and lowered his eyes painfully. The policeman continued: "I, too, have dreamed many times that there's a great treasure buried in a neighborhood in Baghdad, in the basement of a house that belongs to a Mr. X. Do you think I should've given up everything and just gone there?"

The young man heard his name uttered by the policeman in disbelief. To make sure he had heard correctly, he asked him to repeat the name of the person in Baghdad he had just mentioned. When he heard his name spoken again, he was ecstatic but tried not to show it. He begged the policemen's forgiveness and, the next morning, contentedly started making his way back to Baghdad, wondering all the way why he had insisted on taking such an arduous journey, tolerating such hardship and deprivation, to find out in the end that what he sought had been safe in his own home all along!

BIBLIOGRAPHY

Forouzanfar, Badiozaman (ed.), 1994, *Masnavi-e Ma'navi ye Mowlavi [The Masnavi]*, 9th ed., Tehran, Zazeman e Entesharat e Javidan.

Ghasemzadeh, Mohammad (ed.), 1990, *Dastanha-e Masnavi [Massnavi Stories]*, Tehran, Hirmand Publishers.

Nicholson, Reynold A. (ed.), 1992, *The Mathnawi of Jalaluddin Rumi*, Delhi, Adam Publishers & Distributers.

Zamani, Karim (ed.), 1998, *Masnavi-e Ma'navi*, 5th ed., Tehran, Entesharat-e Etela'at.